Everyday Princess:

DAUGHTER OF THE KING

D0008664

...eauty is
...nd from
...thin. The true
...asure of

...eauty is
...termined by
...King of
...eation.

Peaceful House Publishing
3617 N. Georgetown Drive
Montgomery, Alabama

Copyright 2008
ISBN: 978-0-9762140-4-5
Printed in China
Layout and Design Rob Baker

This book is lovingly dedicated to every
young lady who wants to wear
The Crown of Life
one day.
Sheila Keckler Butt

Contents

Everyday Princess:
Daughter of THE KING

This is a book for girls. It is about girls and their relationships. It is about girls and their relationship to God, to each other, and to the world.

When you become a member of the body of Christ, you become a daughter of God. You are a princess in the truest sense of the word, because you become the daughter of the one and only King for eternity! This book will help you live like a daughter of THE KING.

When I surveyed hundreds of teen girls about what topics they would like to study, one young lady wrote, "We want to study about the tough stuff in life . . . drugs, alcohol, death, abuse, eating disorders; things girls often need a chance to talk about but don't ever get. We want to talk about guys, being a strong Christian, and standing up for what's right. We want to find ways to have fun with other Christians."

Another young lady wrote, "We want to talk about dealing with family issues, parents and siblings. We want to talk about dating, healthy relationships, making new friends, keeping old friends, and loving yourself for who you are. We want to be confident and brave and be able to stand for what we believe despite the odds."

I know sometimes it is hard to believe in God. We wonder why He lets so many bad things happen. We wonder why our classmate committed suicide. We wonder why terrorists are trying to kill us. We wonder why young ladies are often mean to each other and say such hateful things. We think about guys. A lot. We wonder what it would be like to be a movie star. What would it be like to have a date with one? At the very least, we would like to be friends with one!

We want to obey our parents but we also want to distance ourselves from them. We want to find out who we really are. We want to do well in school, but we don't want to appear to be too smart and be all about the books.

I know you really want to wear the latest styles and look stunning. I mean, we all want to be noticed, don't we? I am sure that many of you would like to be great athletes or beauty queens. I know many of you have friends who are not Christians but you consider them really nice people. I know you wonder about your future. Will I get married? If so, will I marry a Christian? Will I have a job or stay home? Will I raise children?

Girls, I don't know what your future holds; but I do know Who holds your future! Let's study God's Word together to make sure that we are trusting Him with our future. As one young lady so aptly put it when I asked her what she would tell another young lady who was trying to be a strong Christian, "I would tell her that strength comes from deep within and looking for it is easier for some than for others. Remember, though, for something to be found, it must be sought. Always remember the importance of doing what is right and don't be afraid to ask for help. Strength as a Christian is mighty and the strength is there if you look for it!"

I couldn't have said it better myself! This study will help you find that strength. Another young lady put it this way, "I would probably tell her to stand strong even when she stumbles or falls. I know what it is like to struggle as a Christian and sometimes mess up or make a bad decision, but the most important thing is to keep trying and never, never, never give up!"

Being the daughter of The King will not always be easy. In fact, sometimes it will be hard simply because of your royal bloodline through Christ. There will be daily temptations and tough choices to make. But your Father has left you awesome instructions. Let's study them together!

Sheila Keckler Butt

Meeting The Love of Your Life
Or
"My first love . . ."

Jesus said to him, "You shall love the Lord your God with all your heart, with all your soul, and with all your mind."

Matthew 22:37

His name was J.D. Gilbert. Stan and I picked him up one Wednesday evening after Bible study. It was cold, about four degrees, and this young man was hitchhiking. He was a neat looking young man, dressed in his high school jacket and very polite. I greeted him and we talked for a few minutes. Then I just had to ask: "J.D., are you out on this cold, cold night because of a girl?"

"Yes," he answered, "My girlfriend. We had an argument on the phone a few minutes ago and I am not going to be able to sleep until I see her and talk to her face to face."

Now understand that J.D.'s girlfriend lived about nine miles from where we picked him up. He was going to walk nine miles to talk to her if he had to! Why? Because J.D. thought he was in love. He may or may not have been, but when we are "in love" we do lots of things out of the ordinary!

I remember being "in love" in the eighth grade. His name was Blake Sampson. He was a new student that year, good looking, and an outstanding athlete. I fell "in love" the minute I saw him! (Of course, it wasn't love, but you could not have told me that at the time.) He sat across the hall from me in another classroom directly in my view. I doubt if I ever missed a day of school that year and I was not very happy when he missed a day either. It really burned me up when the teacher closed the door for some reason. You see, the best part of my day was staring across the hall and daydreaming about us having a house, three kids and a pro football contract!

When we think we are "in love," many other things become low priorities in our lives. We will do almost anything for the one we think we love. God knows how we feel about being in love, because He created us that way. And do you know what else? God wants to be the love of our lives. He wants to know that we would walk nine miles to worship Him. He wants to know that we think of Him often and picture ourselves in the future living for Him and bringing others to Him. He wants to know that we love Him enough to glorify Him with our lives. God wants your heart first . . . and then

> *God knows how we feel about being in love, because He created us that way. And do you know what else? God wants to be the love of our lives.*

He will give you the physical blessings of this life. He knows what is best for you, and because He loves you so very much, He will bless you if He knows that He is the ruler of your heart. In Psalm 37: 3-4, we are told, "Trust in the Lord, and do good; dwell in the land, and feed on His faithfulness. Delight yourself also in the Lord, and He shall give you the desires of your heart."

We also sing a song based on Matthew 6:33 which says, "Seek ye first the kingdom of God, and His righteousness, and all these things shall be added unto you."

"If You Love Me, Keep My Commandments"

The things written in the Bible are not there just to make us "feel" good. The Bible contains the promises of God. When teaching a Bible class of young ladies at a Christian school, I had one young lady tell me that her preacher said that the Bible was a "love letter" from God and not a book of rules for us to follow. I totally agree that the Bible tells us of the awesome love of God, but we also know that John tells us in John 14:15, "If you love me, keep my commandments." That sentence literally means "If you love me (you will) keep my commandments." Jesus tells us in John 15: 9-10, "As the Father loved Me, I also have loved you; abide in My love. If you keep My commandments, you will abide in My love; just as I have kept My Father's commandments and abide in His love." This sounds like more than just "feeling like" you are in love, doesn't it?

In 2 John, verse 6, we read, "This is love, that we walk according to His commandments" . . . Love sounds like more than a "feeling" here, too, doesn't it?

The word used in the Bible for the kind of love that God has for us is the Greek word, "agape", which means a sacrificial love. It means that it may cost me something to love you, but I will do it anyway! As a matter of fact, God sent His only son to die for us, even when most of the people Jesus came in contact with scorned and rejected Him.

If we really love the Lord, then we will do what he says. . . not just on Sunday or Wednesday evening. If God's Word is truth, then it is the truth for every day and every minute of our lives. Our heart must not have one set of truths and our minds another.

Do I Love with My Heart or My Brain?

I read recently about a college professor who walked into the classroom and drew a picture of a heart on one side of the blackboard and the picture of a brain (to represent the mind) on the other side of the blackboard. He told the class that some things you believe with your heart and other things you know with your mind. That is just not true if you believe that the Bible is God's Word. You believe it with your heart AND you know it in your mind. A good study of Christian evidences will convince you that it is much more logical to believe in God than in the theories and philosophies of men (Colossians 2:8). We will talk more about that in another chapter.

It may cost you something to love God with all of your heart and mind. You will not be able to be like everyone else and be a part of everything that is going on. When I asked one young lady about her personal struggle with putting God first in her life, here is what she said. "My own struggle is having to sit back and do what God says, instead of participating in certain activities."

Let me ask you this: Is this young lady showing God that she loves Him by her actions? Does she believe what He says is true? You see, her love for the Lord is not just a fleeting emotion, but a way of life. This is what God wants from each of us. He wants us to love Him enough to make tough decisions, (even when we don't feel like it). He wants us to love Him enough to make the right choices (even when we know we would like to do something else). He wants us to love Him enough to be different from the world (even when it would be much easier to be like everyone else). You see, God wants you to "love the Lord your God with all your heart, with all your soul, and with all your mind." God did not put us into this world to "fit in" but to live our lives so that we will be fit for the kingdom of heaven one day.

Am I in Vogue with My Faith or Am I in Love with My Lord?

Another important thing for us to understand is that loving God is a lot more than just a public display of affection. Recently I have noticed Hollywood actors wearing apparel that would make you think they love and appreciate Jesus. For instance, one young male actor in a recent interview was wearing a hat that said "Jesus is my Homeboy." But the fact of the matter is, this young actor currently lives a very immoral lifestyle. How do I know that? How could I not know that? We see, hear or read about him almost daily and nothing points to the likelihood that he is even remotely trying to live a Christian life.

I have seen other movie stars and famous people wearing clothing or jewelry saying the same or similar things, and yet we know many of them are living sinful lives. KNOWING ABOUT Jesus and KNOWING Jesus are two completely different things. The person who understands the true nature of Christ would know that He really is not a homeboy. He is so much more than that! The One I worship, adore and dedicate my life to has to be more awesome than just a neighborhood friend.

Why? What does "homeboy" mean, anyway? In Webster's dictionary there are two meanings. The first is: "from my neighborhood." Now let me ask you this . . . is Jesus from your neighborhood? A careful study of John 1: 1-3 tells us the Jesus is from heaven! He is a part of the Godhead. Jesus was with God in the beginning, created this earth, and will be forever. He is not from our neighborhood.

The second definition of homeboy is: "a member of my gang." Girls, Jesus is not a member of your gang or one of your peers. He would not be a part of any particular group if He was physically here with us today. Do you know why? Because Jesus is no respecter of persons and He certainly would not need a gang to make Him feel like He was a part of something. He is everything!

Are You a Jesus Chic?

I have a catalog in front of me at this moment. The title of one page is "Be in Vogue with Your Faith." This catalog is filled with all kinds of jewelry, notebooks for school, t-shirts, and other items with such logos as "Jesus Chic," "Son Lover," "Jesus is my Homeboy," and many other professions of faith. But what does the Bible tell us in James 2:24? "You see then that a man (Greek word meaning "mankind," which includes women) is justified by works, and not by faith only." James also says in verse 17 of that same chapter, "Thus also faith by itself, if it does not have works, is dead."

"*Trust in the Lord, and do good; dwell in the land, and feed on His faithfulness. Delight yourself also in the Lord, and He shall give you the desires of your heart.*"
Psalm 37: 3-4

Many of these outward professions of faith (public displays of affection) are just an attempt by marketers to make big money. In August of 2005, Reader's Digest ran an article entitled "Selling Faith." It concluded with this statement, "In this age of market evangelism, the ring of a cash register can be sacred music."

Remember that you don't need outward professions of faith when you are living a Christian life. Others will see that you are different and some will want to know why. That will open doors for you to talk to them about the first love in your life.

Keep God's Word in Front of You . . . It Can Give You Strength and Encouragement

Let me add that not everything with a scripture verse on it is only for show. For instance, as I am writing this chapter, I am drinking from a mug that has the scripture, "Now faith is the substance of things hoped for, the evidence of things not seen," (Hebrews 11:1). I did not buy this mug to show the world that I love the Lord. It is for my own personal use in my home. The verse often reminds me to have faith even while doing the boring tasks of everyday life. It is for my edification. By using the mug, I am not trying to prove to others that I love the Lord. Having a scripture on your notebook, on a bracelet or a necklace, may just be a reminder to you and can give you strength and inspiration. Just make sure that others are able to tell that you love the Lord by the way that you act every day.

Make sure that your love for the Lord is not just a public display. People should know that you love the Lord by the way that you live, by your actions, and not because you are trying to be in vogue!

In Matthew, Chapter 15, Matthew tells us how Isaiah describes hypocrisy. He says "These people draw near to Me with their mouth, and honor Me with their lips, but their heart is far from Me" (verse 8). How do people know that we love the Lord? There is only one way that matters. The apostle John tells us, "Now by this we know that we know Him, if we keep His command-ments. He who says, 'I know Him,' and does not keep His commandments, is a liar, and the truth is not in him. But whoever keeps His Word, truly the love of God is perfected in him. By this we know that we are in Him" (I John 2: 3-5). That is the same way your friends and the people in the world will know that you love the Lord. Don't be fooled. Being in vogue with your faith is not the same as being in Christ!

NEWSFLASH:
God Has No Grandchildren!
Your Mom and Dad's Faith is Not Enough . .

Do you know why it is so important that you are learning how to love God yourself? Because God has no grandchildren! Your parents cannot have a strong enough faith to get you to heaven if you do not have faith of your own. Even if your father is a preacher, an elder, a deacon, or if your mother is one of the most faithful servants of the church, neither one of them has enough goodness to get you to heaven.

How do we know that? Many scriptures in the Bible point to the fact that every Christian must believe, repent, confess and be baptized for himself or herself. But for the record, let's look at an Old Testament passage in Ezekiel. In chapter 14, God is talking about destroying a city because of its unrighteousness. In verse 20, we are told that "even though Noah, Daniel, and Job were in it, as I live," 'says the Lord God', "they would deliver neither son nor daughter; they would deliver only themselves by their righteousness."

You see, each one of us can only be responsible for ourselves. When you are busy looking around at all of your peers, please understand that you will stand alone in judgment before God (2 Corinthians 5:10). And so will they. If you decide now to make the Lord and His will the first priority in your life, then many of the other choices you will have to make will become clearer to you. I am not saying all of those decisions will be easy. I am saying that you will know what is right. If you love the Lord, you will be able to say the same thing that Joseph said when he was tempted by Potipher's wife on a daily basis. He did not say, "What will my friends think?" He did not say, "What would my Dad think?" He did not try to rationalize and say, "If I don't do this, Potipher's wife could destroy me," or, "If I don't do this, she will think that I do not like her." No. Joseph said, "How then can I do this great wickedness, and sin against God?"

Don't Lose Your SELF In Your Circumstances!

Joseph knew what it was to love God. Even though he was hated by his brothers, sold as a slave and cast into prison, his love for God never depended on his circumstances. Neither should yours. None of us have perfect circumstances.

If you decide now to make the Lord and His will the first priority in your life, then many of the other choices you will have to make will become clearer to you.

Maybe you do not have a strong Christian home. Maybe your parents fight about money, alcohol or relationships. Don't think that your home is so different from everyone else's. Many of us come from dysfunctional families. We are still accountable to God for what we do with our own lives. Learn to love God with your whole heart . . . and that includes your actions. The Lord will bless you for it. As one young lady commented, "If you love God, NEVER give up. Always try your hardest to please God, not others. Think about what you really and truthfully need and want for yourself, not what others want. It will always lead you to God."

Recently I sent an email to a young lady about her dating status because I wanted to introduce her to a Christian young man. She is a junior in college. Let me share her response with you:

> "Well, about my dating status, I'm single. I haven't dated anyone since the young guy this summer. I just don't think it was the right time for him. He's just really busy, and maybe we just didn't click. We got along great and have the same Christian background which was absolutely wonderful, but I think he wanted that 'chemistry' but I guess it just wasn't really there. So, I've been single and have just been working on my relationship with the Lord and being close to Him and falling more in love with Him and praying that someday He'll provide a loving Christian husband for me when the time is right."

What a beautiful attitude from a Christian young lady who has her life together. She is confident and strong. She has already made up her mind who the first love of her life is, and she is trusting God to send her the second!

Questions
Chapter One

1) The young man, J.D. Gilbert, thought he was in love. The fact is that most people do not marry the person they dated in high school. Since we know that, why should we be careful about thinking that we are "in love"?

2) How can we be sure that God knows how we feel about love?

3) What does God tell us will happen if we make Him the first love of our lives? (Read Matthew 6:33.)

4) The Bible can be called a love story. However, it also teaches us how to live. Read John 14:15 again. What does that mean to you?

5) Is love more than a feeling? Explain. (Read John 15:9-10 and 2 John, verse 6 to help with your answer.)

6) What does the Greek word "agape" mean?

7) Describe sacrificial love. Is it just a feeling?

8) Why is it so hard to "sit back and do what God says, instead of participating in certain activities" as one young lady said?

9) Why is it usually so much easier to be like everyone else?

10) What is an example of a public display of affection? Why is knowing Jesus so much more important than just knowing about Jesus?

11) Read John 1:1-3 and then read John 1:14. What do these verses tell us about Jesus?

12) What is meant by the phrase "God has no grandchildren"? (2 Corinthians 5:10 will help with this answer.)

13) Why should your love for God not depend on your circumstances or what is happening around you? Tell about some people in the Bible who loved the Lord even in bad times.

14) Can you tell if someone loves the Lord and is trying to please Him? How?

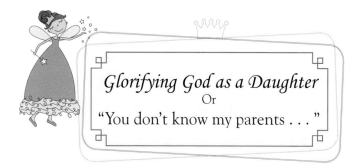

Glorifying God as a Daughter
Or
"You don't know my parents . . ."

"Many daughters have done well, but you excel them all."
Proverbs 31: 29

She kept hanging around after Bible class and I knew something was wrong. I had known Heather since fifth grade and this was the summer before her senior year. She and Kevin had been "going out" since Heather was in ninth grade. He was a fine young man even if he was a little mischievous. I had never worried about them making bad decisions. Today, however, sweet Heather looked defiant. She walked up to me with resolution in her eyes and said, "Mrs. Sheila, I can't live at home anymore. I can't stand another year at my parents' house."

I knew that look and remembered the feeling. I ran away once at about Heather's age. I thought I couldn't stand my parents or that house any longer. But I also remember what a struggle it was to try and go back home and the heart-break it caused me and my family. I knew Heather's parents were good Christian people, even if they were wound a little too tightly. I was sure that everything they did was with the intention of protecting their daughter.

See, we parents don't always get it right. We want to. For the most part, we try very hard to. But we are not always going to make the right decisions. We hold you too tightly or we let you go too quickly. Sometimes we are just not sure what to do.

Heather and I had a long talk. I told her what I have just told you. I advised her strongly not to run away and to stay at home for her senior year. I knew she would be going to a Christian college the next year and then she would have much more freedom as well as responsibility. You see, Heather was ready for that. Her parents were just not ready to let her go. I told her that as long as she lived in their home, she needed to abide by their rules. Heather was a mature young lady. She realized the truth of what I was telling her, even if she didn't like it for the moment.

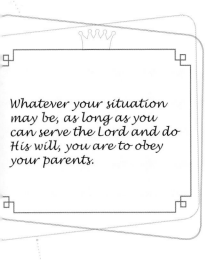

Whatever your situation may be, as long as you can serve the Lord and do His will, you are to obey your parents.

Heather is now married to that faithful Christian young man and has three beautiful children. She has her own home now and can make her own decisions. She can take what she learned from her parents' home and take full advantage of all the good things she learned from her parents. She may also choose to do some things differently in raising her own children.

Heather is very close to her parents now and they are very helpful and loving to the grandchildren. Heather learned something by staying home her senior year. She learned endurance. James tells us in James 5:11, "Indeed we count them blessed who endure. You have heard of the perseverance of Job and seen the end intended by the Lord that the Lord is very compassionate and merciful." Heather has seen the end intended by the Lord in her life, because she obeyed God and honored her parents even though she felt like doing otherwise.

Being the Daughter God Wants You to Be Now Is Great Practice for Your Future!

Learning to glorify God in your life as a daughter is very good practice for many of the other relationships in your life. Do you think Heather will be a better wife because she decided to stay when she felt like leaving her parents' home? Do you think she will be a better member of a congregation because she listened to someone who might have been older and wiser? Do you think her experience will make her a better mother? I hope you said "yes" to all of these things, because the truth is that by staying home Heather learned a lot about lasting, committed relationships. They are not always easy.

We learn from the scriptures that God commanded those in the Old Testament to "Honor your father and your mother; and, he who curses father or mother, let him be put to death" (Matthew 15:4). Do you know that a disobedient son under the Old Testament was to be stoned to death? Read Deuteronomy 21: 18-21. I don't know if many sons were stoned to death and I can't say for sure what happened to rebellious daughters, but I can assure you it was not pleasant! It is not hard to see that obeying your parents and respecting them is important to God. Jesus also told the rich young ruler in Matthew 19, "Honor your father and your mother." I understand that it is sometimes hard to do. If it were easy, God would not have had to repeat it so many times.

Don't Expect Television or the Movies to Show You What a Christian Family Looks Like . . .

Sadly many of our television programs, movies, books and sitcoms totally undermine respect for the authority of parents. The media often makes fathers look ignorant and weak. Many mothers are portrayed as overly concerned with how they look, what neighborhood they live in or their careers. Certainly none of them are trying to show us what a Christian home should look like. We need to go to the Father and His Word for that.

In Ephesians 6, children are told to "Obey your parents in the Lord, for this is right. Honor your father and mother, which is the first commandment with promise: that it may be well with you and you may live long on the earth," (Ephesians 6: 1-3).

Sometimes It's Not What You Think . . . .

Understand that your parents are probably doing the best they can. The way they are parenting you is for the most part, the way their parents taught them. Hopefully, many have learned to take the good things from their past and get rid of the bad things. Whatever your situation may be, as long as you can serve the Lord and do His will, you are to obey your parents.

Sometimes we grow up with misconceptions in our families. We see something differently than it really is. When I was growing up, I just knew that my parents loved my younger sister more than the rest of us children. Of course, they never said that, but when it came time for them to leave the five of us children with a babysitter or a relative, they always left four and took my sister with them. Even if they left for a few days, they always took Nancy. I just took it for granted that they loved her the most and the other four of us learned to live with it.

One day, after having three children of my own, I was talking with my parents and it came up about them always taking Nancy with them. I told them that I always thought they loved her more than the rest of us because she got to go with them. They both got the "deer in the headlight" look. They were stunned! My mother said, "Oh Sheila, we didn't take her because we loved her more. When she was younger she was the troublemaker. We knew we could leave you four without any trouble, but if Nancy was left there would be problems for everyone!"

It's Not Fair!

That discussion was a revelation to me. However, my parents had not taken the trouble to explain this in almost thirty years, so how could I know? Your parents may have a good reason for doing something that seems very unfair to you. If you think something is not fair, you need to talk to them about it, and I mean talk. Don't just mention it and then clam up or go to your room.

Sometimes we think parents are mind readers. I mean, how could they NOT know!? But believe me, most of the time parents are too busy trying to make a living, caring for you and your siblings, teaching you about the Lord, taking care of a house, vehicles, insurance and trying to see that you get to ballgames and practices on time to try and read your mind. You are going to have to make time to talk to them.

The Truth Will Make You Free!

God has commanded parents to be parents and children to be obedient. We need to speak the truth to each other in a loving, respectful way. As Christians, we are commanded to tell the truth. As a daughter, it is very important that you be honest with your parents. If you are truthful, they will trust you so much more. The first time you are caught in a lie, you have damaged their trust in you. Most of the time, it takes a long time to get it back.

I talk to young people everywhere about telling the truth. It will save you tons of heartache and a lot of extra energy and time having to make up stories to cover up the lies you have already told! Even more importantly, your heavenly Father knows when you are striving to please Him by being truthful with others.

Tell the Truth Even When It Hurts . . . You!

One night, I was putting two of my young granddaughters to bed at my house. The youngest one had just started kindergarten. The oldest one, Emma, said, "Bebe, you would be proud of Grace Anne. She told the truth at school today." I started praising Grace Anne and telling her how great that was. Then Emma added, "After she bit that little boy!"

Of course I was surprised, but this was an even better lesson. You see, when we can tell the truth knowing that there will be a price to pay for it, then we know the value of honesty. People will know we have integrity no matter what the situation. The virtue of honesty is very valuable and will earn you mega points in your relationship with your parents. Also, God will know that you are sincerely trying to do His will.

"*I go to my Mom and God. My Mother can listen and give me advice, but if it is something I don't want anyone else to know, I tell God. His advice is the best you will ever find.*"
(*Anonymous*)

We are all human and we all have faults. We need to try our best to love each other unconditionally, as Christ loves us, and live in harmony with our physical family.

Hopefully, some of you are like many of the young ladies I have surveyed. When I asked the question: "Who do you go to with your problems and struggles, and why?" here are some of the answers I got:

"I go to my Mom and my Christian girlfriends. My Mom has experienced what I'm going through and gives me advice and my friends and I can help each other work through things." (Brittany)

"I go to my best friends and my Mom. They are closest to me and I know they love me." (Olivia)

"I usually go to God or my Mom. God knows everything and my Mom has been through things I am going through." (Rachel)

"I go to my Mom and God. My Mother can listen and give me advice, but if it is something I don't want anyone else to know, I tell God. His advice is the best you will ever find." (Anonymous)

Mollie says, "I go to my Mother because most of the time she listens and helps me decide what to do. I also talk to my brother about things because I know they both love me and care about what's going on."

Another young lady said, "I go to my Mom, because she talks things out with me and explains them to me. And most of all, she is always there for me."

As you can see, many of the young ladies I have surveyed over the years have great relationships with their mothers. I have often wondered how different our lives might have been if Eve would have had a mother to talk to in the Garden of Eden, or even a trusted friend to advise her to do God's will instead of her own. Maybe she would not have eaten that forbidden fruit!

By the way, there were several young ladies who said they talked to their fathers. If your Dad is a good listener and can give good advice, be sure to keep the lines of communication open with him.

Choosing to be the kind of daughter God wants you to be now will help you be the kind of Christian, wife, mother and friend that will bring glory to God for the rest of your life.

So You Think You Have the Answers . . . This Young Lady Knew She Didn't!

One thing that has always intrigued me about Queen Esther in the Old Testament is that she listened to other people who were wiser than she was.

First, look at Esther 2:15, "Now when the turn came for Esther the daughter of Abihail the uncle of Mordecai, who had taken her as his daughter, to go in to the king, she requested nothing but what Hegai the king's eunuch, the custodian of the women, advised. And Esther obtained favor in the sight of all who saw her."

Do you see what is happening here? Esther was smart enough to realize that Hegai would know what the king wanted in a woman. She did not try to do everything her own way, but may have dressed like he advised, possibly used the perfume he advised and maybe even approached the king as Hegai advised. She listened to him and did what he said. Many times, young ladies, listening to someone wiser than you is the smartest thing to do!

Even after Esther became queen, she still understood that she needed to listen to the advice of her cousin, Mordecai. In spite of the fact that she could have been killed for going in to see the king without being called, she followed the advice of Mordecai who had raised her as his own. In so doing, she saved a nation.

We often think of Esther as a strong, courageous woman, which she was, but we should also remember her as being smart enough to listen to others who could give her good advice. If she had not listened, she might not have become queen and she might have perished with the Jewish nation.

Let me share a couple of other responses from girls about who they go to with their problems and struggles:

"I go to my Mom or someone at church like my teachers because I can trust them and I know they will help me with my struggles." (Anonymous)

27

" I go to God. He knows what's best. He made the map of your life. He knows what obstacles are to come and prepares you for your trip." (Whitney)

Love Them Because You Love Him!

I understand that being the daughter that God wants you to be in your physical family is sometimes a struggle. Sometimes we have brothers and sisters to contend with. Sometimes we have parents that we think speak a different language than we do, or at least are living in another time frame. Remember, however, if you are a Christian, you are a daughter of God first. You need to honor, respect and obey your parents because He tells you to. Forgive their mistakes, just like they are to forgive yours. Don't lie to them. Be where you say you are going to be.

Your parents or guardians are trying to help you make the best choices now and for your future. It won't be very long until you are making your own choices. Choosing to be the kind of daughter God wants you to be now will help you be the kind of Christian, wife, mother and friend that will bring glory to God for the rest of your life.

You Mean the Son of God Had to Obey His Parents?

Jesus is a great example to us in learning this lesson. He knew that He was the Son of God but He also knew that God wanted Him to be in subjection to His earthly parents. Do you remember the story in Luke 2, when Jesus was left behind in Jerusalem at the Feast of the Passover? His parents thought He was in the company of relatives and acquaintances. Maybe they thought He was walking along with His cousins who were about His age.

At any rate, after a day's journey when they could not find Him, they returned to Jerusalem to find Him sitting in the middle of the teachers in the temple.

We find out that He was teaching the teachers and that "all who heard Him were astonished at His understanding and His answers" (Luke 2: 47). When His parents asked Him why He had done this to them, He answered, "Why did

> "Whatever your family situation is, if you will love the Lord and honor and respect your parents, it may be said of you, "Many daughters have done well, but you excel them all."
> Proverbs 31: 29

you seek Me? Did you not know that I must be about My Father's business?'

At the age of twelve, Jesus knows that He is the Son of God. Because of that, we might think that He had only to be subject to God, but that was not the plan. We learn, as the story continues in verse 51, that Jesus left the temple, went with his parents to Nazareth, and was subject to them. Being subject to them means that He obeyed them. He willfully obeyed His parents even when He realized that Joseph was not His real father and that He was the most powerful person in this world! There were many wonderful things that were going to happen in the life of this young man. But for that time in His life, He was to be subject to His parents.

Every one of us at one time or another is in the same position. In order to be pleasing to God, even His own Son had to obey His earthly parents while He was a young man. In the Book of Romans, Chapter 1, being disobedient to parents is listed with every sin imaginable including murder and hatred of God. Of course we wouldn't murder anyone or profess to hate God, but why do we think it is more acceptable to disobey our parents? The truth of the matter is . . . it is not more acceptable to God!

But I Want to Know What God Has Planned for Me!

Sara Grace, one of the young ladies I talked to, described her struggle like this: "I have a hard time waiting to see what God has in store for me. I'm too anxious to know where I'm going and am not content enough with the present." I am sure many of you have felt the same way.

There is a beautiful song we sing that could be your theme song for the next few years. It will help you and give you strength to "keep on keeping on" believing the Word of God and living it while many of your friends are making bad choices.

TEACH ME LORD TO WAIT

Teach me Lord to wait
Down on my knees
'Til in your own good time
You will answer my plea.

Teach me not to rely
On what others do
But to wait in prayer
For an answer from You.

Those who wait upon the Lord,
Shall renew their strength,
They shall mount up with wings
Like eagles . . .

They shall run
And not grow weary
They shall walk
And not faint.
Teach me Lord,
Teach me Lord,
To wait.

I can almost guarantee that if your parents know that you are trying to glorify God in your life that you can wrap them around your finger! They will respect your thoughts and trust you because they know you are ultimately trying to please the Lord. Whatever your family situation is, if you will love the Lord and honor and respect your parents, it may be said of you, "Many daughters have done well, but you excel them all" (Proverbs 31: 29).

I can assure you from the lives of hundreds of young ladies that I have witnessed through the years . . . the Lord will bless you for it now and in the future!

Questions
Chapter Two

1) Have you ever felt like running away from home? If so, why? What happened when the prodigal son decided to leave his home?

2) In James 5:11, we read about perseverance. What is perseverance? Why is it important for you to have perseverance (especially in your walk with the Lord)?

3) Did Job know what the end of his life was going to be like? Read James 5:11 again. Do you think that the end intended by God for Job's life was different than the end intended by Satan? Could that be true for you? What will decide the end of your story? (John 12:48)

4) Do you think that the way we handle the relationship with our parents is any indication of how we will handle the relationship with our husband and maybe even our own children one day? Why?

5) How do we know that honoring (respecting and obeying) our parents is important to God?

6) Will most television programs, songs, sitcoms and news that we hear daily help us understand what a Christian home should be like? Why or why not?

7) Is it possible that parents may have a good reason for doing something that you do not understand or that you think is unfair? What should you do if this is the case?

8) Why is it so important to be truthful with your parents? Does it help the atmosphere at home if your parents trust you? How?

9) What do you think might have happened if Eve had a mother who believed in God and Eve had been able to talk with her before making her decision to eat the forbidden fruit?

10) Is it important for you to forgive your parents' mistakes? Why?

11) How old was Jesus when He got left behind in Jerusalem? Did He understand who He was then? How do we know?

12) What does the Bible mean when it tells us that Jesus was subject to His parents?

13) Read Romans 1: 28-31. Notice that being disobedient to parents is on this list of things that are "not fitting." Why do you think that is?

14) Why is it so hard to wait to see what God has in store for your life?

15) Write down one thing you struggle with in your relationship with your parents. If you would like to, share it with the class.

Glorifying God in My Body
Or
"Am I beautiful?"

"Or do you not know that your body is the temple of the Holy Spirit who is in you, whom you have from God, and you are not your own? For you were bought with a price; therefore glorify God in your body and in your spirit which are God's."

I Corinthians 6: 19-20

One of the most important ways we can glorify God is by reflecting our love for Him in the way we dress and how we treat our bodies. The way we present ourselves to the world every day should let others know that we understand that we are daughters of The King.

What Are You Fishing For?

I like to fish. I have known several girls who like to fish, too. I asked my husband to dig a pond for my Christmas present a couple of years ago. He had someone come and dig up about an acre of our yard for a pond and now it is full of water and fish. One of my favorite things to do is sit at that pond and fish. Right now, the fish are small. I use different kinds of bait to catch different kinds of fish. I have one kind of bait for blue gill, one kind of bait for large mouth bass and another kind of bait for catfish. I call the catfish bait "stinky" bait. (I guess you can figure out why!) None of the other fish will bite it. No matter how many times I throw it in on my hook, I will only catch a catfish. Sometimes I look at Christian young ladies and wonder what kind of fish they are trying to catch by the way they dress.

You see, there are lots of young ladies who say they love the Lord and want to marry a fine Christian young man someday, but they dress like they are trying to catch a longing look from lustful eyes. They dress like the world (because it's the trend) and then wonder why the worldly guys make off-color remarks to them and about them. Never forget that what you wear is a reflection of your heart and mind. Don't be surprised if you get bitten by the wrong kind of fish if you are using his favorite bait!

Sometimes I look at Christian young ladies and wonder what kind of fish they are trying to catch by the way they dress.

The Bible gives us a lot of instruction on how we are to present ourselves to the world. Don't think for one minute that it is outdated. Do you think God knew you were going to live in this time and this culture? Of course, He did! And in His Word He gives us timeless advice on how to dress.

Would You Put a Beautiful Gold Ring in a Pig's Nose?

Let's pretend that the most beautiful young lady you have ever seen walked into the room right now. She is absolutely stunning! There is not a person who wouldn't say she is gorgeous. Let's say, however, that she is wearing a pair of very short shorts and a halter top. Do you know what she looks like to the Lord? She looks like a very expensive ring in a pig's nose! How do I know that? Look at Proverbs 11: 22. It says, "As a ring of gold in a swine's snout (a pig's nose), so is a lovely woman who lacks discretion." What is discretion, you ask? Webster's Dictionary says discretion is " The quality of being discreet (prudent, cautious, careful about what one says or does); one who takes caution; liberty or power of acting with one's own judgment (rather than following the crowd or the trend) ; the quality of being careful."

Discretion in our dress means that we will be modest and carefully dressed using our own judgment about how we want to look instead of following the style and trends which show every curve of our body and often too much cleavage and skin. If a beautiful young lady is immodestly dressed, she looks like a gold ring in a pig's nose to the Lord! God gave her beauty (exemplified by the gold ring) but she is squandering it by trying to look like the world!

One day when I was working at the church building, three young ladies from the youth group came into my office. They had on short shorts and some pretty tight tops. When they saw me they said, "Oh, Mrs. Sheila, we're sorry. We know we should not be wearing this in the church building." Do you know what my reaction was? "If you are going to be wearing those clothes at all, it better be in the church building!" At least in the church building the men are trying to keep themselves pure and unspotted from the world. At least the men in this building are making an effort to block out the constant barrage of sex and immodesty in the world and would try very hard not to look lustfully at these young ladies. But let me ask you this: Are the men you see at ballgames, in the grocery store, in the mall, at the arcade, at the library or at the movies so concerned with keeping their lives pure? I can tell you that, for the most part, they are not. And they really don't care about helping you keep your life pure, either!

What's She Trying To Catch?

Not long ago I was standing in line at the mall, waiting for a Cinnabon (hoping for lots of icing) when I noticed the young lady standing two people in front of me. She was probably 18 or 19 years old. She had on extremely tight and low cut jean capris with her back showing down to the top of her you know what. She was wearing a top that looked like it had come from Victoria's Secret, her breasts hanging out leaving nothing to the imagination. She was wearing lots of dangling jewelry and bling. I can tell you that for a good ten minutes, as we stood waiting, many men, young and old cut right through the people in our line and looked her over with lustful eyes. For some reason, I felt sorry for her. She was using the wrong kind of bait and attracting the wrong kind of men. Sure, she was getting plenty of looks, but I can tell you that these men were not thinking that they would like to marry her and have her raise their children! As a matter of fact, I would say that some of them were already married and some of them were over twice her age.

Please understand that God knows what is going on in the world. He lets people make choices. You may say, "Well, I can't help how boys and men think." I can tell you this. You can help how they think about YOU! Not only do we want our clothing to reflect our love for the Lord, we would never want to cause others to sin because of what we are wearing.

In Proverbs 2: 11, we are told "discretion will preserve you." In other words, being discreet (modest) in how you dress may save you from some very bad situations.

During a church leadership camp for young men and women held every year at Freed-Hardeman University, a survey was passed around the boy's dorm. It asked what the young men considered to be modest clothing for girls. One of the boy's comments about the girls was this: "If she will let you see it, she will let you touch it!"

One young man added this comment, "If girls want to be liked for who they are and not their bodies, then they should try dressing modestly."

Another young man stated, "Wake up! We guys may be responsible for our own actions, but if you don't want guys staring at your body, then why are you wearing those tight jeans? You can no more wear tight jeans and expect guys not to stare than you can wear a cherry pie on your head and expect people not to laugh." (Ron, 17)

What Do People See When they Look at You?

How you present yourself to the world by the way you dress is one of the ways in which you teach people how to treat you. That's right! You actually teach people how to treat you by the things you do and the clothes you wear.

When I was in high school, I was not a Christian. However, when a classmate cursed in front of me, they would often say, "Sorry, Sheila, I forgot you were standing here." Truthfully, I had never said anything about their cursing. But I didn't curse and so it made them uncomfortable to curse in front of me.

For another example, I didn't drink either. I often dated boys who may have been drinkers, but they did not drink when they were with me. Why? Simply because by my actions (actually by NOT doing those things) I was showing others how I expected to be treated.

In my manner of my dress, however, I might have been telling the world that I was someone I was not. Let me explain . . .

Something happened one day in a class that made me start thinking the way I dressed was not reflecting my heart. When I was a freshman in college, I sat next to a very nice young man in chemistry. I picture him as being a doctor now or in some type of research. He was the studious type. We got to be good friends. One day he said to me, "Sheila, you are a tease." I was surprised and a little hurt. "What do you mean by that, Grant?" I asked. "Well, it's the way you dress," he said. "You dress like you are ready and willing for whatever might happen, but you really are a nice girl."

Is the "In" Style Your Style?
Your Own Style Should Reflect Who You Are!

That was a shock to me! But it was the truth. I dressed in whatever was in style. If the style was short skirts, I wore them. If it was tight jeans, I wore them. If it was in style, I thought it must be O.K. This friend of mine had opened my eyes to the fact that I might be attracting the wrong kind of guys. Believe me, I took it to heart! Yes, I was offended at first; but the truth was . . . I knew he was right. I also knew that he was really my friend to be that honest with me. Proverbs 27 tells us that the wounds of a friend (something that may hurt) are better for us than the kisses of an enemy (something that may seem good to us at the time).

Never forget that what you wear is a reflection of your heart and mind. Don't be surprised if you get bitten by the wrong kind of fish if you are using his favorite bait!

I realized that because of the way I was dressing, I was in danger of ending up with someone who really did not care a flip about me as a person. I did not want to date guys who were just out for what they could get. I wanted to show on the outside what kind of person I really was on the inside. I began changing my wardrobe.

Picture This!

Look at your wardrobe. Look at pictures of yourself. What do you see? Do you see a young lady who is reflecting a love for the Lord in her dress or do you see someone who is buying into the trends and styles even if they are not modest?

It would be hard for me to believe that you don't know if something is modest or not. When I was watching a woman's volleyball game with our four-year-old grandson, he commented, "Those ladies aren't wearing enough clothes." If he knows what modesty is, I am sure that you do!

I was recently at a teen devotional at the skating rink. There were probably a hundred teenagers there. We sat on the floor of the skating rink "Indian style" and I can tell you that I got an unwelcome view of the rear ends of many young ladies! If I was getting that view, you can bet many others were, too. When you are trying on and buying clothes, maybe you had better sit on the floor, bend over and then reach around and get a feel for what might be "mooning" the people behind you if you buy those particular jeans!

Let me share with you a few questions to ask yourself about your clothes:

1) Will what I am wearing glorify God? (1 Corinthians 10:31; Exodus 28:40; Isaiah 61:3; 1Timothy 2:9,10).

2) Am I modest according to God's standards? (Genesis 3:21; Exodus 20: 26; 28: 40-43). Would I feel comfortable with Jesus standing next to me?

3) Will my clothing hurt or help my influence for the Lord? (Romans 13:10; 15:3; Philippians 2:3-4).

4) Is it too short? (Be sure to sit down, cross legs, reach up and then decide).

5) Is it too tight? If I get too cold, would my breasts reveal my temperature?

6) Is the neckline too low if I have to bend over to get something?

7) If sleeveless, are my underclothes showing?

8) Can you see right through it? Am I encouraging someone to lust after me, causing him to sin? (Romans 14:13; I Corinthians 8:9; Matthew 5:27-28).

9) When I come to worship am I dressed respectfully and appropriately? Is it possible that I show my respect or disrespect for my God and my brothers and sisters in Christ by the way I dress?

10) Am I dressing to let the world know that I am choosing to be chaste (pure and holy) or that I want to be chased by worldly men?

If you are flaunting your body in public, you are snubbing your nose at a God who loves you more than anyone on earth ever could! Don't be afraid that you might look different if you take these suggestions to heart and dress for the glory of God. There are plenty of other young ladies who have gotten tired of letting the world dictate to them how they should dress. One young lady, Ella Gunderson, became frustrated trying to find fashionable modest clothes so she wrote a letter to Nordstrom's department store.

Here is what she said,

> "*I am an eleven-year-old girl who has tried shopping at your store for clothes (in particular jeans), but all of them ride way under my hips, and the next size up is too big and falls down. I see all of these girls who walk*

around with pants that show their bellybutton and underwear. Your clerks suggest that there is only one look. If that is true, then girls are supposed to walk around half naked. I think you should change that."

Guess what? Nordstrom's listened! Here is their reply to her:

" Your letter really got my attention. . . I think you are absolutely right. There should not be just one look for everyone. This look is not particularly a modest one and there should be choices for everyone."

Consequently, Nordstroms introduced a new line of clothes for young ladies that has been described as very feminine and modest. This one young lady made a difference by choosing not to go along with the world. You can, too. If you would like to do an Internet search for modest clothing, you will be pleasantly surprised to find that there are many more young ladies just like you who do not believe that they have to wear the latest immodest styles and trends to look beautiful!

A Beautiful Bride

Recently a Christian young lady went shopping for her wedding dress. She began to get discouraged because there were so few modest dresses. She found the perfect dress and was disappointed that it was strapless. To her surpise the sales clerk told her that they could add beautiful straps to any dress in the store. She got her beautiful, modest wedding dress and looked like a real princess on her wedding day!

Sure, she was getting plenty of looks, but I can tell you that these men were not thinking that they would like to marry her and have her raise their children!

Don't Destroy the Temple!

There is another important reason for us to understand that our bodies are the temple of the Lord. Over the years that I have taught young ladies, I have encountered many young ladies who have injured their own bodies. I have known (and know at this time) many young ladies who are anorexic or bulimic. I have known young ladies who cut themselves, burned themselves and bitten themselves. I am sure that you know girls who are doing those things, too. It is my prayer that you are not one of them. Since at least one in every four young ladies is involved in something like this, I can imagine that some of you are either hurting your bodies with your eating habits, by depriving your body of food, or by physically hurting yourself.

Studies have shown that the most common reasons that young ladies hurt themselves are either to try and get a reaction from someone, to get control of a situation or to stop bad feelings. A book has just been published by Vanessa Vega, who began hurting herself at the age of four. She began cutting herself, then breaking bones and eventually strangling herself. That's when she knew she needed help. Her self-injury had progressed over a twenty-year period. At this point she was about to kill herself. She said that her self-injury gave her an emotional release. She used it to vent frustration, anger and even joy. When she was asked why she injured herself, she said, "I don't have an answer for that. I just finally knew I had to get help."

I can remember sticking straight pins through my skin a few times as a teenager. I just wanted to see how much pain I could stand. I remember hitting the tops of my legs with a coat hanger just to see how big of whelps I could make. It seemed to make me feel better after a bad day at school.

I also dieted many times during my college years and by the time I got married, my periods had stopped. You see, I was gradually heading down the road to destruction, but thankfully, I took another path in adulthood. Many young ladies get on that road and are never able to get off. Don't be one of them.

Ana or Mia Wants to Control You!

The young ladies I have met with eating disorders started out just trying to control their intake of food. Most have ended up with Ana (anorexia) or Mia (bulimia) controlling their lives for many years and perhaps for their entire lives. Some have what is called EDNOS (Eating

Disorders Not Otherwise Specified), which is a broad category that includes basically any obsession with food.

Many times we use an eating disorder or self-injury as a defense against what is going on in our family, at our school or in our relationships. It seems to be a way of our getting in control, but in reality it will cause us to be totally out of control if we continue doing it. It can eventually destroy our relationships and our lives.

I have met women in their 40's who have been struggling with some kind of eating disorder for most of their lives. I knew one lady who had been bulimic for over 20 years and her vital organs just finally shut down. She left a husband and two daughters grieving the loss of their wife and mother. I recently read of a young woman whose husband was leaving her after 11 years of marriage because he said she loved her bathroom scales more than she loved him.

What Scales Do You Love?

Not long ago I told a young lady on the phone that she needed to get rid of her bathroom scales. I told her that she was weighing her life on the wrong scales. Do you know what her comment was? "But Mrs. Sheila, I love my scales. I couldn't live without my scales!"

When I went to a public school counselor to tell her that I was taking one young lady from her school to an eating disorder clinic, she told me that she had thirty other young ladies that she wished I could take, too!

When we are overly concerned with our own weight, we also tend to judge others based on their weight, too. Often if someone is thinner, we will be jealous. And if someone weighs more than we do, we often make them feel uncomfortable around us. How sad that is! Every one of us is made in the image of God and no matter what we weigh, we are very, very valuable human beings! Anyone who judges another young lady by the size of clothes she wears is making a bad mistake. It is good to eat healthy and to exercise, but we need to make sure that we don't define ourselves or other people by what they weigh. There are many things that contribute to a person's size including heredity, medication and metabolism. Only a very shallow person judges a person by how they look.

Just recently, Seventeen Magazine started a campaign to help young women appreciate their bodies. It is called the Body Peace Project. The object of the project is to get young ladies to sign a contract saying that they will not abuse their bodies and that they will be comfortable in their skin. What does that tell you? It tells you that even Seventeen Magazine recognizes the danger of a culture obsessed with body images.

> "What shall we say then to these things? If God is for us, who can be against us?" God is on your side. He wants you to win over anything that is hurting your body. He will help you overcome it.
>
> Romans 8:31

God Made You Beautiful!

There is great freedom in realizing that God made you in His image and you are beautiful! Ask God to help you change your attitude about how much you weigh and how much other people weigh. Ask Him to help you not to judge your self-worth or the worth of others based on what the scales show. You see, the bathroom scale is not the standard by which we should be measuring our lives. The scale that we need to be using to measure our beauty and worth is the Word of God. The Bible says that the most beautiful thing that a young lady can have is a gentle and quiet spirit. Let's see what Peter tells us about beauty, "Do not let your adornment be merely outward, arranging hair, wearing gold or putting on fine apparel, rather let it be the hidden person of the heart, with the incorruptible beauty of a gentle and quiet spirit, which is very precious in the sight of God," (1 Peter 3:3-4).

Eliab was Hot but His Heart was Not!

Let's look at what God told Samuel about Jesse's son, Eliab. When Eliab came before Samuel, Samuel was impressed by his appearance. "So it was, when they came, that he (Samuel) looked at Eliab and said, 'Surely the Lord's anointed is before Him!' But the Lord said to Samuel, 'Do not look at his appearance or at his physical stature, because I have refused him. For the Lord does not see as man sees; for man looks at the outward appearance, but the Lord looks at the heart" (1 Samuel 16: 6-7).

Eliab must have been tall, dark and handsome! Certainly Samuel judged him by his great looking appearance, and in doing that, he made a mistake. Many times, we do the same thing. Let's not be guilty of judging ourselves or others by using the wrong scales!

Your Body . . . A Dust Bunny Some Day?

Kim Alexis, a famous model for many years, told in a television interview that many, many nights she ate only a head of lettuce for dinner. She talked about how she had abused her body over the years. She then made the comment that she does not want to be remembered for her body because her body is just going to be dust one day. We know that all of our bodies are going to be dust one day (Genesis 3:19). She said that she wants to be remembered for her attitude of heart, for being a good mother, for giving something back to the world and for loving Jesus.

God Is on Your Side!

The truth is that when we love the Lord, we give Him control of our lives and we learn what He wants us to do through His Word. We learn that our body is His temple and we are never to intentionally harm it. We are to let God control how we use our bodies to His glory. With His help and the help of Christian friends, (including some adults in your congregation) you can face any problems that you may be having in your life. Don't be afraid to let someone know you are struggling. Romans 8:31 says, "What shall we say then to these things? If God is for us, who can be against us?" God is on your side. He wants you to win over anything that is hurting your body. He will help you overcome it.

Questions
Chapter Three

1) How can the way we dress reflect our love for Jesus?

2) Do you know girls who are using the wrong bait? Why would they do that? Remember, if it is not on sale, don't advertise it!

3) Read Proverbs 11:22 again. What does it mean?

4) What is discretion? What does it mean to be discreet?

5) Can you help how guys think about you? How?

6) In Matthew 5:14 we are told that Christians are the light of the world. Why does that sometimes make people in darkness uncomfortable? Read John 3: 19-21 and I Peter 2: 9-10. What do these verses tell us?

7) How can you tell if something is modest or not?

8) What impression are you giving others if you are flaunting your body in public?

9) In what ways do young ladies often injure their own bodies?

10) Three kinds of eating disorders are mentioned in this chapter. What are they?

11) What problems can eating disorders cause for your body? What problems can they cause in your mind?

12) Why would we judge another person by her weight? What would be wrong with that?

13) What standard should we use to judge our own beauty and self-worth? Why?

14) Read 1 Peter 3: 3-4 and 1 Samuel 16: 6-7. What do these verses tell us about how God views our beauty and self-worth? How is this different from what we see and hear from people in the world and the media?

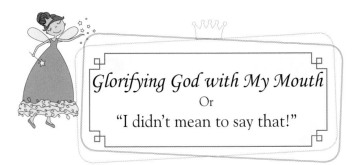

Glorifying God with My Mouth
Or
"I didn't mean to say that!"

*"In the multitude of words sin is not lacking;
but he who restrains his lips is wise."*

Proverbs 10:19

It was one of the happiest mornings of my life! It was my eighth grade year and I had just been elected cheerleader for the first time ever that day! I was your "average" girl in middle school. Not really pretty, not a genius, not much money . . . already certain that I was not going to get a car for my sixteenth birthday and pretty sure that I would never be Homecoming queen. I did have parents who loved me, but honestly, they knew very little about the viciousness of middle school culture. They actually believed that most of the girls my age were "nice."

As I was walking down the hall, I was still dazed that I had been elected cheerleader. Glancing down, I saw a note on the floor. I instinctively (or out of curiosity) picked up the note and read it. It was from one of my "friends" to another one of my "friends." This is what the note said . . .

"I don't know how Sheila Keckler ever got to be a cheerleader. She isn't pretty and she doesn't have nice clothes!"

After reading that note, do you know how I felt? Have you ever read something like that about yourself? Have you ever written something like that about someone else?

Just finding that note in the eighth grade took much of the joy out of my next few years of school. You see, up until that time, I really had not worried about whether I was pretty or not. And I certainly was not overly concerned about my clothes. But do you know what happened? For a long time after that, I became very self-conscious. Do you know what that means? It means that I constantly worried about my looks and my clothes. I always thought the other girls were looking at me to find something wrong.

The Terrible Toos!

Unfortunately, I had reverted back to the "terrible toos!" I started doing something that psychologists call "impression monitoring." I started worrying about what everyone else was thinking about me and watched them closely to see what their impression of me was.

And when I thought about it, I could always find that I was too short, or too stout, or too timid, or too average, or too fair skinned, or had hair that was too dark, or had too many freckles . . . and the list went on. I was living the "terrible toos" just because of some thoughtless comments made by one young lady to another. I think there are many young ladies living with the terrible toos and that attitude takes a lot of joy out of their lives.

Let me warn you right here that anything, and I mean anything you say will probably be repeated.

Now let me ask you a question. Do you think the girls who wrote that note lost any sleep over it for one day? Probably not. You see, there are now, and always have been, girls who do not mind hurting you with what they say. In the book Queen Bees and Wannabes we learn that many girls (Queen Bees and Sidekicks) use "emotional violence" to belittle other girls and to maintain their position in the social order.

I know that you understand the social order at your school and sad to say, possibly even in your youth group if it is very large. I am quite sure that you know where you fit in (whether you are happy with it, or not). But do you understand the importance of the things that you say?

Let me mention here that I never did confront my so-called friends about this note because I had never been really close to them. But do you think that I ever counted either of them as my friends anymore?

Possibly, one of them might have been sorry if she had realized that I read the note. But the truth is after you have hurt someone like that, there is a real chance that you will never be friends again. You may still speak to them, but any real opportunity for a long term friendship is probably lost. And possibly, if you have said or written something bad about another girl, you may have lost the chance to make a really good friend!

"A Little Bird Told Me . . ."

Let me warn you right here that anything, and I mean anything you say will probably be repeated. You may think that you have a great friend right now who would not repeat anything you say, but many times those things just "slip." Maybe even a bird will tell what you said.

Look at Ecclesiastes 10:20 . . . "Do not curse the king, not even in your thought; Do not curse the rich, even in your bedroom; For a bird of the air may carry your voice, And a bird in flight may tell the matter."

This verse is warning us that anything we say will probably be repeated! How much better not to have to worry about what you have said about another person!

I know this is not easy. I know you see grownups (even Christians) saying things about others that they should not say, but the truth is, you are only accountable for yourself and the only words that God expects you to control are your own.

When one of our sons was in seventh grade, I heard him talking to one of his friends about a mutual friend of theirs. I heard my son call the young man a "sissy." I knew that would come back to haunt him, I just didn't know how quickly! Within ten minutes after he had hung up, the phone rang. It was the "mutual friend" who had already been told that my son called him a "sissy." Our son learned a valuable lesson that day. I am glad that he learned it early. It is my prayer that you will learn it, too. It will save you a lot of grief and keep you from saying things that you may regret later.

Let me share with you something written by an someone who understands the danger of gossip:

MY NAME IS GOSSIP

I have no respect for justice,
I maim without killing,
I break hearts and ruin lives,
I am cunning and malicious,
and gather strength with age.

The more I am quoted,
The more I am believed.
I flourish at every level of society.
My victims are helpless.

They cannot protect themselves against me,
Because I have no name and no face.
To track me down is impossible.
The harder you try,
The more elusive I become.

I am nobody's friend.
Once I tarnish a person's reputation,
It is never the same.

I pit people against each other,
For the purpose of controling others.
I shrewdly imply that I know more than I actually tell.

I spawn suspicion, and generate grief.
I make innocent people cry in their pillows.
Even my name hisses . . . .
I AM CALLED GOSSIP.
(Anonymous)

One young lady wrote to tell me about her struggle with gossip. "I often find myself gossiping with my friends . . . I mean it is SO easy to say something and the worst part is, the more you gossip, the easier it becomes."

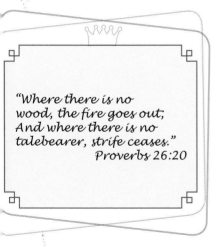

"Where there is no wood, the fire goes out; And where there is no talebearer, strife ceases."
Proverbs 26:20

Where There is No Wood . . . The Fire Goes Out!

Most of us understand where this young lady is coming from. But do you know that the Bible tells us how we can stop gossip in its tracks before it spreads? Read Proverbs 26: 20. It says "Where there is no wood, the fire goes out; And where there is no talebearer, strife ceases."

You see, if no one spreads the gossip, it would soon die out. And you have the ability to make it die. Make a decision that you are not going to gossip!

So how do we control our tongues? In the book of James, we learn that it is a very hard thing for anyone to do, but we also learn that God expects us to try to control what we say. James, the brother of Jesus, says that the things we say are like a fire that cannot be put out and once the spark is lit, a ravaging fire may begin!

Your Heart Can Be a Bridle For Your Tongue!

James also says, "If anyone among you thinks he is religious and does not bridle his tongue but deceives his own heart, this one's religion is useless" (James 1: 16).

Have you ever ridden a horse? If you have, then you know that the bridle helps you direct the steps of the horse. If the horse has been trained properly, then the rider uses the bridle to let the horse know which way to go. In the same way, your heart should bridle your speech. Your heart should let you know when to speak and when to be quiet. The trouble is that we often blurt something out before we take the time to listen to our heart. Your heart should be the bridle that controls your speech, especially if you love the Lord!

Girls, do you understand this? Read James 1:16 again. This verse says that you cannot truly love the Lord and talk badly about other people!

Now open your Bible and read James 3:1-12. What is this passage telling us? It tells us that we are to work very hard at controling our tongues. Look at verse 9, "With (our speech) we bless our God and Father, and with it we curse men, who have been made in the similitude of God.

Out of the same mouth proceed blessing and cursing. My brethren, these things ought not to be so."

If She's the One Who's Jealous
Why Does It Hurt Me So Much?

One thing that we learn from this passage is that we are to be kind to others. Maybe you don't like the personality of another girl. Maybe you are jealous in some way of another girl. Maybe someone has been unkind to you and you just want to "even the score." Perhaps someone is jealous of you for trying to be more like Christ. A jealous person can hurt someone very much. The Bible warns us about jealousy and teaches us that jealousy is a very hard thing to overcome. "Wrath is cruel and anger a torrent, but who is able to stand before jealousy?" (Proverbs 27:4).

Jealousy is often cruel and unfair and God recognizes that. But please let me assure you of this. One day, our God will "even the score." You do not have to spend your time worrying about "payback." You do not have to spend your time defending yourself against false accusations. You see, the light will shine through the darkness.

On any given day, you may feel down and depressed because of what someone has said about you. However, let me GUARANTEE you this . . . if you will be a strong enough person to keep your mouth shut, you will be stronger for it, the other girls will respect you for it, and God will be glorified for it! The person who talks behind another person's back will be found out. Proverbs 11:9 tells us: "The hypocrite with his mouth destroys his neighbor, but through knowledge the righteous will be delivered."

This verse says that a hypocrite may try to hurt you, but the truth about how you live your life will come to light. The way you live each day will prove the liar wrong. Proverbs 20:11 says, "Even a child is known by his deeds, whether what he does is pure and right."

Am I a Hypocrite?

Now the question for each of us to answer is this, "Am I a hypocrite?"

Your first answer is undoubtedly, "No. I would never want to be a hypocrite!" But truthfully ask yourself, have you been a part of destroying someone else by the things you have said about them?

You might not have really meant to hurt them. You might have just been adding something to an already hurtful conversation. But why would you even take part in hurting someone else?

Proverbs 21:2 says, "Every way of man (or young lady) is right in his own eyes, but the Lord weighs the hearts." God knows WHY you say what you say. God knows your motives for every word that you speak. He knows your heart.

In 1 Corinthians 4:5, the Bible tells us that the Lord "will both bring to light the hidden things of darkness and reveal the counsels of the hearts." God knows your motives for talking about another person and those motives will not always be hidden.

As a young girl, you should begin asking the Lord to guide your thoughts and your speech for the rest of your life. Your prayer, as well as mine, should be:

"Search me, O God, and know my heart; Try me, and know my anxieties; and see if there is any wicked way in me, and lead me in the way everlasting" (Psalm 139: 23-24).

That verse should reflect our heart's desire. Your life at school, at home and as an adult woman will be more blessed when you learn to choose your words wisely and know that the Lord will strengthen you and give you wisdom. Before saying anything, you may want to ask yourself the simple question, "What would Jesus do?"

Proverbs 29:11 tells us that "A fool vents all his feelings, but a wise man holds them back."

Proverbs 11:19 tells us "In the multitude of words sin is not lacking, but he who restrains his lips is wise."

And we also learn from Proverbs 17 that people may believe that you are much smarter than you really are when you say nothing at all!

"Even a fool is counted wise when he holds his peace; when he shuts his lips, he is considered perceptive." Proverbs 17: 28

Also, remember that you may be able to stop something very hurtful just by saying nothing. "Where there is no wood, the fire goes out. And where there is no talebearer, strife ceases."

Never Wrestle with a Pig . . .

There is an old Chinese Proverb that says "Never wrestle with a pig. You both get dirty and the pig loves it!"

There are some girls who thrive on keeping things stirred up. They thrive on talking about each other and carrying messages about each other. They are happy when someone else is hurt, because that either makes them look better or keeps them one step ahead of someone else in the social order of things. But make no mistake. That kind of girl is getting dirty and she may even appear to be enjoying it, but one day, as she matures, she will see the filth and dirtiness around her and wonder what happened.

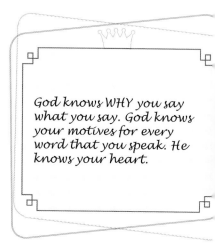

God knows WHY you say what you say. God knows your motives for every word that you speak. He knows your heart.

Even if she repents one day, and we pray that she will, much of that dirt will leave a stain on her life and the lives of others. The last thing we want to do is wrestle with a pig!

"It Just Slipped Out . . . "

Another lesson we learn from James, chapter 3, is that we cannot profess to love God with our lips and then curse, swear, and use the Lord's name in vain and be pleasing to God. Others should know that you love God, by what you say, and just as much by what you don't say! "Out of the same mouth proceed blessing and cursing. My brethren, these things ought not to be so" (James 3:10).

Can you imagine our Lord using curse words? Can you imagine Him gossiping about anyone? Look at Isaiah, chapter six. Read it and you will see that Isaiah could not be used by God until he cleaned up his mouth! When Isaiah realized that he was in the presence of God, he said, "Woe is me, for I am undone! Because I am a man of unclean lips, And I dwell in the midst of a people of unclean lips."

Young ladies, we live in a nation of unclean lips. Our television programs, movies and music are full of curse words and unwholesome speech. Unless you decide right now that your speech is going to be different, people will never believe that you are an authentic Christian. They will never see Jesus in you. In Isaiah 6:8, you will see that Isaiah was ready to say, "Here am I, send me," only after he cleaned up his mouth.

"Cool Outfit!"

The Bible talks about another kind of speech which the Lord hates. It is called "flattery." What is flattery? It is the opposite of gossip. Gossip is saying something behind someone's back that you would never say to their face. We have already discussed many of the pitfalls of gossip. Now let's turn our attention to flattery. Flattery is also condemned by God. Flattery is saying something to someone's face that you would never say behind their back. But what do I mean by that?

Let me give you an example: One day Emily comes to school with a really odd looking outfit. Secretly you laugh at it behind her back, but to her face you say, "That outfit is really cool." Flattery is lying. Flattery is saying something that you don't mean. And just like gossip is a sin, flattery is a sin.

I know we don't hear the word "sin" spoken much anymore, and none of us like to think we are sinning. But sin is what separates us from God. A malicious tongue and a flattering tongue will keep us out of the presence of God, perhaps for eternity.

Consider this: "A lying tongue hates those who are crushed by it, and a flattering mouth works ruin" (Proverbs 26:28).

"He who goes about as a talebearer reveals secrets; Therefore do not associate with one who flatters with his lips" (Proverbs 20:19).

Why would it be wise not to be known as a person who flatters other people? Because the one characteristic that would stand out above all of your other characteristics would be insincerity. Who wants to be known as an insincere person? Certainly one who flatters others will get that reputation and before long even sincere compliments and praise will be worthless.

People may even think you are flattering them in order to make them look bad. And maybe you are. Proverbs 29:5 says "A man who flatters his neighbor, spreads a net for his feet." Remember, the Lord knows our motives.

Does that mean we should never tell someone how nice they look or what a great thing we think they have done? Of course not. And you know better than that. However, we learn from the Bible is that our praise and compliments need to be genuine or they are wrong.

You may have seen adults practice flattery and it may have temporarily made someone feel good. However, a person who insincerely flatters others will be seen for what she is. Be honest, kind and sincere in your praise and encouragement. God will bless you for it and you will be a blessing to others because of it!

Above all, remember that the Bible tells us that we will all be judged by the words we speak. One day, we will give an account for everything we have said (Matthew 12: 36,37).

You may remember this verse of one of my favorite children's songs:

Oh, be careful little lips what you say,
Oh, be careful little lips what you say,
For the Father up above is looking down in tender love,
Oh, be careful little lips what you say!

God was listening to Isaiah every day of his life. And He is listening to you and me. "Oh, be careful little lips what you say!"

Questions
Chapter 4

1) Would you consider most of the girls in your middle school or high school "nice?" Why or why not?

2) Have you ever found out that one of your friends talked badly about you behind your back? How did that make you feel?

3) What does being "self-conscious" mean? What is wrong with being too self-conscious?

4) Do we sometimes lose the chance to have a really good friend because of something we have said? How could that happen?

5) Read Ecclesiastes 10:20 again. What do you think that verse means?

6) Read Proverbs 26:20. What does this verse tell us about gossip?

7) What does the bridle do when a person is riding a horse? How should our hearts be the bridle for our words? Why is this so hard for us sometimes?

8) Read Proverbs 27:4 again. Have you known someone who has been hurt by jealousy? Without giving names, relate to the class what happened. Why do

you think the Bible tells us that it is hard for someone to stand up against jealousy?

9) Read Proverbs 20:11 again. What does this verse say about your life?

10) Does God know your motives for talking about someone else even if you are pretending to care about them? Why is it important for you to understand that God knows your motives? (See Proverbs 21:2 and 1 Corinthians 4:5).

11) The old Chinese Proverb says: "Never wrestle with a pig. You both get dirty and the pig loves it!" What does that mean to you? Do you know young ladies who love to stir up strife? Why should you not join them?

12) Read the entire chapter of Isaiah 6. How did Isaiah feel when he realized he was in the presence of God? What did he say about his speech? How does that relate to us today?

13) What is flattery? Why do you think the Bible condemns flattery?

14) How could flattering someone make them look bad? Do you know girls who insincerely flatter others and then talk about them? Why would a young lady who loves the Lord not want to be known as someone who insincerely compliments others?

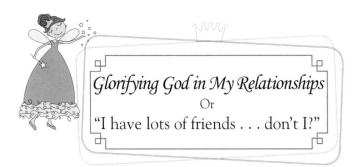

Glorifying God in My Relationships
Or
"I have lots of friends . . . don't I?"

"A man of many companions may come to ruin,
but there is a friend who sticks closer than a brother."
Proverbs 18:24 (ESV)

Sandi had two friends she liked better than anyone else. They had been friends since second grade and the three of them entered junior high this year. Her friend, Kelly, was sweet and quiet. Sandi enjoyed spending time with her. Kelly did not have many friends because she was shy, but Sandi had always appreciated her sincerity and loyalty and they had been "best friends" in elementary school. Sandi could tell Kelly anything and she knew Kelly would not repeat it.

Her other "best" friend Jenni, on the other hand, was generally the life of the party. Jenni knew how to have fun and make others laugh. You could tell that Kelly enjoyed being around Jenni, too, probably because Kelly was so shy she seemed to be captivated by Jenni's comfort in being "center stage." For most of their elementary school years, the three girls were inseparable.

Junior high was different. There were a lot more girls now and the three of them changed classes often. Sometimes they were visiting with other girls from a previous class and had very little time for each other between classes. Most of the time they did not get to sit together at lunch. Sandi began noticing that Kelly stood and talked with Jenni a lot more now. As a matter of fact, she was becoming Jenni's shadow! She would often see her friend, Jenni, in the middle of a group of girls laughing and talking and there would be Kelly right by her side! Sandi was beginning to feel excluded. It seemed like more and more girls liked Jenni and she didn't have much time for her old "best" friend anymore. It looked like Kelly was happy just being a part of the group. Sandi just wanted the three of them back the way it used to be. As the year progressed, Sandi realized that her friends had moved on. She was sad and hurt. Why couldn't it just be like it used to be?

As a matter of fact, our relationships during our school years will make us have some of the happiest days of our lives and make us have some of the most miserable days.

It is natural for Sandi to want to keep her relationship with Kelly and Jenni. God made us girls to enjoy relationships and to long for strong, lasting relationships. Those are the very characteristics that make us wonderful wives and mothers when that time comes in our lives. However, during the teenage years, this same longing for relationships can hurt us very much. As a matter of fact, our relationships during our school years will make us have some of the happiest days of our lives and make us have some of the most miserable days.

You May Think So Now . . . But Twelve Years Is Not Forever!

One important thing for us to realize in our relationships with other girls in school is that most of those relationships will not last. I am sure this is not what you want to hear, but let me tell you from experience that if you have one, two or three really good friendships in your lifetime, you will be blessed! True friendships are built on honesty, sincerity and trust. Building a strong friendship takes time. However, let me remind you that any good relationship is built on friendship. That includes your relationships with boys.

Most of the relationships we have in school are due to the fact that we spend so much time together. The young people in your classes may not be the ones you would choose to spend so much time with, but because of schedules and circumstances you are together a lot of the time. Most of these young people will just be acquaintances. We will define acquaintances as people that you know a little about, spend some time with, talk to briefly, but never really relate to on a deeper level. Your school years will be filled with acquaintances. Because you are a young lady who loves the Lord, you need to be kind to all of your acquaintances. A genuine smile will go a long way. You should look for opportunities to invite them to your congregation and to youth activities. Always make sure that they see you living an authentic, sincere Christian life.

Let me share some thoughts with you from a young lady named Kelli. I asked her to speak to a group of ladies and teenagers about being a young Christian in high school today. Here is what she shared:

"I am seventeen years old. I am a senior in high school and I am a Christian.

It's extremely difficult to be a Christian, first of all, but to be a Christian teen is an even more difficult feat. And I know because I am going through it right now.

I go to a public school and it is especially difficult because I have all kinds of peer pressure pushing me down all the time. I see obscene behavior at school every day. And I hear the use of God's name in vain, I can't even count the number of times, every . . . single . . .day.

And I know the way I get through it every day is because God is watching over me. I mean, at school, I know exactly where I can go to get marijuana, ecstacy or any other drug I could want. I know where all the parties are every weekend, if I ever wanted to go, and I even have a few friends who want me to go with them. Instead, I have friends over to my house every other Friday for a movie night and dinner because I know the only way we'll make it through those weekends is being together and knowing that God is watching over us.

School is one thing but society and the media are another. I am going off to college this fall and I pray that God gives me the strength to keep walking that narrow path. I've noticed how society and even some "so-called" Christians in society have become completely tolerant of just about every lifestyle these days. There really isn't a need for the word "tolerant" anymore; it's almost become a cliché.

For example, it's so hard to watch "prime-time" television, or a movie or even read a teen magazine without premarital sex being glorified. As if teenagers didn't have enough already with hormones, sex is thrown in our faces everywhere we look on a daily basis. It is so hard to stand up to these temptations. I know God sees all of this and the only way I will keep resisting and staying pure is because He is watching over me."

I am sure that many of you can relate to Kelli. She understands how important it is for her not to take part in many of the things going on in her school. Kelli understands that one of the worst things she could do is to change who she is in order to be accepted.

Bad Habits Are a Lot Like the Flu . . . They Are Contagious!

Studies have shown over and over that girls who run around with girls who drink alcohol are much more likely to become drinkers. Girls who hang with girls who smoke are much more likely to begin smoking. And listen to this closely . . .studies have shown that girls who watch a lot of "prime-time" TV are much more likely to have pre-marital sex!

I think Kelli understands a lot about friendship, the world and the media. Her real friends are the ones who come to her house for dinner and a movie . . . not the ones who are encouraging her to party with them. She sees the world trying to draw her into sin and she is not counting on the media to tell her the truth about life!

I am also sure that Kelli is a great example for the girls that she spends the most time with. Most of your friends and acquaintances right now are teenagers who are trying to decide what they are going to believe and who they want to be one day. Now is the time to share your faith with them. I do not mean that you have to cram it down their throats, but you need to be ready when problems arise in their lives with the truth of the scriptures. There are many girls who are not ashamed of being a part of the Gothic culture, being sexually active or being in the "Out and Proud" club. Why should you be ashamed of being a Christian when you stand for what is right, truthful, lovely and eternal?

Do Not Be Ashamed of Jesus . . .

The Bible warns us about being ashamed of Jesus Christ. "For whoever is ashamed of Me and My words in this adulterous and sinful generation, of him shall the Son of Man be ashamed when He comes in the glory of His Father with the Holy Angels (Mark 8:38). DO NOT BE ASHAMED. Your life, your words and your actions may be the ONLY way many of your friends and acquaintances will ever see Jesus and be drawn to Him. Don't miss this opportunity to show them what Jesus has done for you and what He can do for them!

I always had a lot of acquaintances in school but only one or two real friends. On the outside, I looked like I had it all together. I was voted "Friendliest" my senior year. I was friendly to everyone regardless of their social status and I know

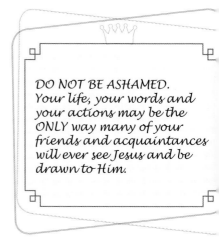

DO NOT BE ASHAMED. Your life, your words and your actions may be the ONLY way many of your friends and acquaintances will ever see Jesus and be drawn to Him.

that they appreciated it. I spent many nights at home with my family because I did not party with the party crowd and I was not a Christian. I did not have a "youth group" or a youth minister. I didn't even have a congregation of people who cared about me! But I knew who I wanted to be. And I knew that I wanted to like the person I saw in the mirror every morning.

I was not the only one who held strong beliefs in my high school although I often felt like I was because I had no Christian friends. The couple who were elected Prom King and Queen our senior year were Christians and they went to the dance, had their pictures made and left. They were not popular because they could dance. They didn't even want to dance. They were popular because they were good.

Right now I am challenging you, young ladies, to be good. When I became a teenager I told myself that I did not want to drink, do drugs, smoke, or have sex outside of marriage and I meant it. During the teen years, you are actually in the process of becoming the person you want to be some day. Make the choices and choose the relationships that will strengthen the decisions you have made about the person you want to be in a few years.

We are often so concerned with what other people think of us that we don't realize that what we think of ourselves and furthermore what God thinks of us far outweighs anything that our friends at school think of us! Let me remind you again that this is only a few short years of your life, but your choice of friends can make a profound difference on how you will spend the rest of your life.

A Tragic Story of Friends . . .

Let me tell you Eli's story. I had Eli in my Bible classes occasionally for a couple of years. Eli was a wonderful, handsome young man full of personality. He was about 12 when I first met him. He came to Bible camp one year and was baptized. When he was with his Christian friends, you could not have asked for a nicer guy. It was always "Yes, Ma'am" and "No, Ma'am." He enjoyed his Bible lessons. He wanted to do everything right. His parents were divorced and we only got to see Eli and spend time with him when he visited his dad who was a member of our congregation. When Eli was at his mother's house, however, he had a completely different group of friends. One night, when Eli was with this group of friends, one of them decided he needed some cash. They robbed a convenience store and the clerk was killed. Eli was with the wrong group. He was convicted and sent to prison with the rest of the group.

They aren't a group anymore. They have all been sent to different prisons and will lead totally different lives.

Eli was in the wrong place with the wrong group. He has been in prison for several years now. This sweet, handsome young man who could have had such a bright future is spending his days and years in prison. When I wrote to him, he realized his mistake, but the life he had chosen simply by being with the wrong group was taking a toll on him. The last time I went to visit him, he had been moved to another prison because he had been involved in a fight. He made the tragic mistake of picking the wrong group to hang with.

One young lady in my class put it this way, "I would tell a young lady who is trying to be a strong Christian to really be careful about who you hang out with because that can make a huge difference." What a sad difference it made in Eli's life!

Don't Worry . . . Be Happy
God Has Great Plans for You!

Don't worry too much that most of your relationships will just be acquaintances for now. You may be blessed with one or two true friends. Did you notice the verse in Proverbs that we put at the beginning of this chapter? The verse says that a man (or girl) of many companions may come to ruin. Why would that be? Because the truth is that many people are really just interested in what you can do for them. They are not really interested in what is best for you! Lots of girls will act like they are your best friend, but when it comes right down to it, they will do what is best for them or what will put them in a better standing with other girls and guys rather than think about what is best for you. Maybe you have even been that way with other girls before and treated them badly. As you mature, you should begin to care more about others and less about yourself. I hope you are getting there. **JOY** comes from putting **J**esus first, **O**thers second and **Y**ourself last. The Son of God was a perfect example of someone who experienced true joy by giving Himself for others (Hebrews 12:2).

Characteristics of a Good Friendship

After you have been around another girl for a while, you may decide that you would like to develop a deeper friendship with her. Real friendships are not made in a week. Real friendship takes time and commitment and the only way to have a really good friend is to be one yourself!

In order to have a friend you can trust, you need to be a friend that someone can trust. In order to get respect from a friend, you need to respect your friend.

Don't miss the opportunity to show your friends what Jesus has done for you and what He can do for them!

If you have a good, true friend, then you need to learn not to let little problems between you become big problems. Here are four important things that will keep that from happening:

1) Do not keep something inside of you, stewing about it, and letting it make you madder and madder.

2) You need to talk about the problem.

3) You must not "blow up" but talk about it calmly and sincerely. Your body will warn you if you are about to say some things you shouldn't . . . your heart will beat faster, your face will begin to blush, you may find it harder to breathe or you may start shaking. Listen to your body. Get out of that situation and discuss it later. If you try to talk about it then, you will regret it.

4) Sometimes you have to agree to disagree; you need to respect your friend's opinion but make sure that yours is respected, too, or she is not a true friend.

There may be times in your life that you do not have a really close friend. Pray about it. Talk to God about it. He knows what you need. During these times, remember that you have a Heavenly Father and that there are people who genuinely care about you.

Let me share with you how some Christian girls handle their relationships:

"When I have problems and struggles, I go to God because you don't ever have to try to get in touch with Him, He is always there waiting on you to talk to Him and I know that I have His full attention and that He will help me do the right thing."

"When I have problems and struggles, if my prayers do not soothe my thoughts, I often go speak with elders' wives from my congregation . . ."

"When I have problems and struggles I go to my parents because they know me and they've been through it before . . . "

"I go to my sister and my mom . . ."

"I go to my parents and God . . . they are the people I trust the most."

"When I have problems and struggles, I go to an older teenager who is a role model and I ask how she would handle it. And I go to God in prayer because I know that He will help me."

Bad Days and "Pop Up" Ads . . .

Understand that God knows you completely. He knows your strengths and your weaknesses and He has a plan and a vision for you. This is a great time to really begin experiencing God and developing a relationship with Him.

We all know that some days are great and other days we wish we could have a "do over!" We know that we are moody and emotional sometimes and so are all of the other girls our age. Sometimes there is a biological reason for our moodiness. Our bodies at this time are constantly changing. Some days we are very confident and some days we believe that there is nothing really good about us. We think that maybe in our case God really did make some junk!

We need to look at these bad days just like the pop up ads on our computer. We can be enjoying working on the computer when all of a sudden a silly pop up ad will appear and we have to click on it to get it off of the screen before we can continue. Well, some days and some things that happen to us are like that. They momentarily derail our confidence and catch us off guard. In order to be the best that we can be, we need to understand that these are just temporary "pop ups" and not let them define who we are. On those days and at those times we need to make an extra effort to be kind to others and to ourselves. The truth is that you are still a wonderful, awesome work in progress!

A young lady gave this advice to her struggling Christian friend: "Surround yourself with good Christians. Get to know more Christians your age. God will always be there for you even when nobody else is."

Jesus is your best friend. He gave His life for you. He has promised you that He will never leave you nor forsake you (Hebrews 13:5b) . . . even on those "pop up" days! If you will be His friend in return, your life will be abundantly blessed!

Questions
Chapter 5

1) Have you ever had a time when you and some of your friends had to "move on" like Sandi, Kelly and Jenni? How did that make you feel?

2) Is it natural for girls to want good relationships? How can that be a blessing to us, especially later in our lives?

3) Can you relate to Kelli's story? How?

4) Why should a young lady not change who she is to be accepted? Do you know young ladies who have done that? Why is it especially important for a young lady who loves the Lord not to change who she is just to be accepted?

5) Read 1 Corinthians 15:33. According to this chapter, how have many studies shown that this is true?

6) Why is it so important to tell other teenagers about Christ when the opportunity arises?

7) Read Mark 8:28. It may be easier to deny Christ at this time in your life, but why is it so important not to do that? How does Ecclesiastes 12:1 relate to you?

8) Why is it important to like the girl you see in the mirror? How can you insure that you will always be able to look at yourself in the mirror and not be ashamed of what you are and who you are?

9) How can your choices now help you become the person you want to be?

10) We often think that what people think of us is important. Why is what we think of ourselves even more important? Why is what God thinks of us the most important of all?

11) Have you known someone like Eli who was influenced by his friends? Why is that so tragic? Could Eli's life have been totally different? How?

12) There are many young people who are looking out for themselves and really don't care about you. How would you recognize that in a person?

13) When you have a really good friend, how can you keep little problems from becoming big problems?

14) How can a bad day or a bad incident be compared to a "pop up" ad on your computer screen?

15) How can Jesus be your best friend? What characteristics of Jesus make Him a really good friend to you? How can you be a friend to Him?

Glorifying God in My Recreation
Or
"What's a girl to do?"

"Remember now your Creator in the days of your youth . . ."
Ecclesiastes 12:1

Jessica always loved playing basketball. Even now, she remembers those cold Saturday mornings during the winter months at the gym when she was only in the first grade. Her dad was the coach. They enjoyed those mornings together, eating doughnuts, going to the games, being with her friends. She thinks her mother must have a hundred videos of her games over the past nine years! She may be asked to play on a traveling team next year. Only the best players are invited. Many times there are college scouts at the games, and she always thought she might go to college on a basketball scholarship. This could be her chance to get noticed!

The traveling team practices late on many Wednesday nights and Jessica knows that it is going to be hard not to miss Bible study some of the time. The team often travels on the weekends and she knows that the team travels on many Sunday mornings or Sunday evenings. She is already wondering how she is going to handle it. Her parents have not brought up the question, but Jessica has always loved the Lord and tried to do the right thing. She is concerned about how she is going to accomplish this juggling act.

Taylor began participating in beauty pageants when she was three years old. She always had a beautiful smile and a sweet disposition. At first, she just dressed up, walked out on stage, smiled and answered a question. Her dresses were beautiful! Her mom would put lip gloss on her and everything! On those nights, she felt like a princess!

As Taylor got older and she continued to take part in beauty pageants, her parents realized that she needed to develop a talent for the talent competition. Taylor began playing the piano. She didn't necessarily like all of the practicing, but her talent served her well and she continued winning all kinds of titles. Then, in junior high, the standards of dress changed. Now there was the sportswear competition. Taylor and her parents were happy when they could find pretty, modest sportswear. Taylor and her parents had decided a long time ago that she would only be in pageants in which she could dress modestly. At seventeen years old she won her county pageant. Now she was going to represent her county in the Miss North Carolina pageant! However at this stage of the competition she and her parents realized that Taylor was going to have to wear a swimsuit in front of thousands of people.

Everyone told her that she had a fantastic chance of winning! How could she NOT do this?

Jeni started cheerleading when her older brother, who was nine, was playing football. Jeni was only five. She loved putting on that cute uniform and cheering for him! Her picture album is full of pictures of those years. Jeni kept on cheering right through elementary school. Now she is in junior high. She is considering going out for the middle school cheerleading squad. Of course, she never wears her skirts as short as those cheerleading skirts, but it seems to be O.K. if you are a cheerleader and its "game day." Plus she would never dream of standing in the middle of that gym floor and dancing in front of the whole school with a bunch of strangers watching, but obviously it's easier if you are a cheerleader and dancing with a group. I mean, how could that be wrong? Everyone else does it! She has even noticed the cheerleaders at one of the Christian schools do the same thing. It must be all right.

> *. . . many young people think that they have plenty of time to put the Lord first in their lives. But not right now.*

Jessica, Taylor and Jeni all started out simply enjoying some form of recreation. It could have been softball, dancing, gymnastics, bowling or soccer. Recreation is defined by Webster's dictionary as "refreshment in body or mind, as after work (or school), by some form of play, amusement or relaxation. . . . any form of play, amusement or relaxation used for this purpose, as games, sports, hobbies, reading, walking, etc."

The problem comes when our recreation makes it hard for us to be girls who are glorifying God. The word "glorify" literally means to "magnify." One of the best ways that other people learn about Christ and the Word of God is by what they see in our lives. It is very important to make sure that when people look at our lives, they see that we really are putting the Lord first. Is that going to be hard? Sometimes. Are you going to have to be different? Sometimes. Let's look at each of these three girls and see how she might handle her situation so that she can be an example to those around her and show the Lord that she chooses to serve Him, not just on the Lord's Day, but with her whole heart and on every day of her life!

Jessica's Dilemma . . .

Jessica is going to have to make a decision and she is going to have to talk with her parents about it. Obviously they have supported her many years and most likely will continue to support her in whatever decision she makes. She knows there is a verse in the Bible that says something about not forsaking the assembling of the Christians. The verse actually says this: "And let us consider one another in order to stir up love and good works, not forsaking the assembling of ourselves together, as is the manner of some, but exhorting one another, and so much the more as you see the Day approaching" (Hebrews 10:25).

What exactly does that mean? The Greek word for assembly here means the public worship of the church. (Barnes Notes) The command is to meet together for worship and it is important for Christians to do it. It sounds like there were Christians in the New Testament who were choosing to do other things when the Christians were assembling, and Paul is warning them not to do this! It is possible that they were afraid of meeting with the Christians because they might have been caught and persecuted. It is also possible that they simply had other things they would rather be doing. You see, I am sure that they enjoyed recreation, too. The early Christians had their own games, their own ways to have fun and their own distractions. You see, it is no different just because you live a few hundred years after them. There will always be people who say that they love the Lord and His church but not more than their recreation!

Is It O.K. . . . for Now?

The question for Jessica really is this, "Are you going to put the Lord first or is your basketball really more important for now?"

I have added the words, "for now" in that question because many young people think that they have plenty of time to put the Lord first in their lives. But not right now. There are two very good reasons not to think that!

The first reason is that God wants you to put Him first now! How can we know that? A very wise man tells us in Ecclesiastes 12:1 to "Remember now your Creator in the days of your youth, before the difficult days come . . ."

We can find many great examples in the Bible of young people who loved the Lord enough to make sacrifices for Him. Joseph loved the Lord in spite of years of heartache and imprisonment. Samuel was taken by his mother at a young age to serve the priest Eli. In 1 Samuel 17: 33, King Saul calls David a "youth" when David tells the king that he will fight the giant Philistine, Goliath. We know that Josiah was eight years old when he became king, and "he did what was right in the sight of the Lord" (2 Chronicles 34:3). Remember that Jesus was only twelve years old when He was separated from His parents for three days. When they found Him, He asked them, "Why did you seek me? Did you not know that I must be about my Father's business?" And remember, Mary, the mother of Jesus was not much older than you when God entrusted His Son to her care. We know that the young Mary trusted God completely. When the angel Gabriel told her that she was going to be a mother, even though she had never been with a man, Mary said, "Behold the maidservant of the Lord! Let it be to me according to your word." Mary obviously put God's will first in her life no matter what anyone else would think . . . including Joseph, the man she was engaged to marry!

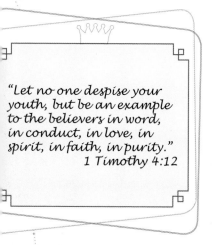

"Let no one despise your youth, but be an example to the believers in word, in conduct, in love, in spirit, in faith, in purity."
1 Timothy 4:12

In the New Testament Paul reminds Timothy that he was taught the Scriptures from an early age by his mother and grandmother, (2 Timothy 3:15). Now read 2 Timothy 1: 3-7 two or three times. In verse 6, it sounds like Timothy might be wavering from preaching the Word. Could it be because he was so young? Paul tells him in verse 7, that God had given him a "spirit of power and love and of a sound mind." He has given you the very same thing.

In I Timothy 4:12, Paul tells Timothy, "Let no one despise your youth, but be an example to the believers in word, in conduct, in love, in spirit, in faith, in purity." God expects you to do the same thing. What a great example you can be for old and young people alike when you decide not to put your love for sports above your love for the Lord. Jessica has the opportunity right now to show others that the Lord is the first love of her life. The truth is that a few short years from now, it will not really matter whether Jessica played on the traveling team or not. And we do not even have the assurance that Jessica will live many more years. You see, one of my dear friends had a sixteen year old daughter who was killed in a car accident on her way to a ballgame recently. Thankfully, this young lady was a wonderful Christian example to many of her friends. When Jessica makes her decision, she needs to understand that God expects her to be faithful in her youth and that we have no guarantee of another day.

Is Taylor Beautiful . . . In God's Sight?

Now what about Taylor? What will she decide? She has spent many hours of her life either in beauty pageants or preparing for them. She has the opportunity now to win the Miss North Carolina pageant and go on to be Miss USA. Her little brother is autistic. Maybe she could even become a spokesperson for autism! Think how much good that might accomplish. And, after all, it's just a bathing suit! Hundreds of thousands of people wear them. Wouldn't it be all right just this time?

Let me share a personal story with you. I did not become a Christian until I was twenty years old. During the time that I was studying the Bible and making many choices, I was asked to be on a television show with a very well known celebrity. To say the least, I was excited about it! I went to the Channel 5 television station in Nashville, TN, auditioned for the part, and got the job! During the audition I was asked to wear a very immodest outfit and I was O.K. with that. After the audition, it took several months to get the program produced. In the meantime, I became a Christian.

One afternoon I was shopping at the grocery store and met one of the elders from the congregation that I had been attending. I remember standing in front of the dairy counter talking to him and thinking to myself, "I wish I had more clothes on."

And then I went home and reviewed my audition tape. I was embarrassed at what I was wearing. You see, for the first time I realized that God cared what I looked like! I realized that I wanted people to know that I loved the Lord and I could not wear that outfit in public. I called the TV station and asked them to find someone else for the part. There went my chance for fame! To think I might have been a movie star! However, the truth is, I realized as I studied the Bible that God is always present and there is no excuse for immodesty no matter how big the prize is! What God prizes is "the hidden person of the heart, with the incorruptible beauty of a gentle and quiet spirit, which is very precious in the sight of God" (I Peter 3: 4).

Do you know what rationalizing means? It means trying to find good reasons for doing something we know is not right. While there may be some good reasons for doing something, there is never enough reason to do something we know is wrong in the sight of God. When we put our recreation before our Lord, we are making a mistake, no matter what the prize may be!

Let me show you an example of a young lady who is rationalizing. I asked several girls what they would most like to be when they grow up. Here is one answer: "I would most like to be a pro basketball player. I would get to play basketball, make lots of money and if I am famous I could get God's Word out better."

Do you see any problem with that kind of thinking? Maybe not at first glance, but I wonder how many worship services and Bible studies this young lady is going to have to miss in her quest to become a pro basketball player? I wonder if her friends will see her as a person who is dedicated to Christ or to the basketball court? I daresay that in her efforts to become a pro basketball player, she would lose much precious time in service to God and with other Christians. It sounds like this young lady is rationalizing. She is trying to believe that her love for basketball, money and fame are things that could glorify God.

Many times you will hear people say "God has given a person a certain talent, so they should use it." In many cases that is true, but in many cases it is not. If you have a talent for something that is wrong or something that will draw you away from the Lord and the body of Christ (the church) then it will not glorify Him. For instance, if you have a talent for stealing . . . would God want you to use it? If you have a talent for lying . . . does God want you to use it? Do you understand the point here? Just because you have a talent for something does not mean that it will be a blessing to you or to anyone else unless you use your talent as God would want you to.

Satan can and will use ANYTHING to draw us away from God, even things that we could call "blessings" such as above average abilities, friends, and material things. We know that Satan can disguise himself and his motives as something good (2 Corinthians 11:14).

Which Crown is Most Precious?

Now Taylor is going to have to decide which crown would be most precious to her. You see, she might win the crown of Miss North Carolina. She might eventually be crowned Miss USA. She might even get to become a spokesperson for autism. But both of these beauty crowns are temporary and she would have to be displeasing to the Lord to compete for either of them.

Maybe by winning the beauty crowns she could be helpful in the campaign to cure autism, but there are many other ways she can serve her cause without compromising her modesty.

If Taylor trusts the Lord and believes His Word, she will one day win a crown! God assures her of that in Revelation 2:10, when He says, "Be faithful until death, and I will give you the crown of life." Notice that He does not say "a" crown, but "the" crown. My prayer for each of you as well as myself, young ladies, is that we will all be beauty queens. We will be beautiful in the sight of our Lord and we will wear THE crown of life forever!

Jeni is Reconsidering . . .

Jeni, on the other hand, just wants to be a cheerleader. There is something special about being popular enough or good enough to be a cheerleader. Being a cheerleader generally means that you were voted on by your class or you are very good at gymnastics and cheering or you were selected by a committee to represent your school. Most people would think that there could not be anything wrong with just being a cheerleader. Honestly, I used to think the same thing. When I was a cheerleader in high school, I can tell you that there

Just because you have a talent for something does not mean that it will be a blessing to you or to anyone else unless you use your talent as God would want you to.

was nothing immodest about our uniforms. As a matter of fact, most of our blouses had long sleeves and there were only about three inches of our legs showing below the knee between the hem of our skirt and the top of our bobby socks. (You can picture this, I'm sure . . .)

Also, when I was a cheerleader, it was very important that you cheer in as deep a voice as you could muster and make your words as choppy as your movements. We practiced that all of the time. We looked and sounded more like robots than dancers in a nightclub!

When our oldest son was in high school he dated a wonderful young lady for two years. She was beautiful on the inside and out. She was a cheerleader at one of the neighboring high schools and as she got older the skirts got shorter and the moves got more seductive. One evening we were playing their school in basketball. It was halftime. Her cheerleading squad began their halftime show. It was very suggestive and revealing. After the halftime, she came and sat by me. She was almost in tears. "I didn't feel good doing that routine in front of Stan and all of these people in this gym," she said. The next Monday she turned in her uniform. She is still a very beautiful young woman on the inside and out. She has a wonderful Christian husband and three precious children that God has entrusted to them. Do you think she has ever regretted that she made the choice to value her purity, wholesomeness and goodness above her popularity? I know she hasn't. And I know that she has given many other young ladies the courage to make good decisions about their recreation. She is someone that God can use to His glory. And you can be, too, by the decisions you are making right now about your recreation. After all, Romans 8:31 says, "If God is for us, who can be against us?"

I would like to close this chapter with a story about a young lady who made wise choices about her recreation. It is written by Jack Carter.

What do you do for fun?

Several years ago a very sweet Christian girl told me about an incident with a young man who had been asking to date her.

He was not a member of the church, and they just didn't have anything in common. She had turned him down twice, and now she said "no" to attending a rock concert with him.

In mock exasperation the young man asked, "What do you do for fun? You don't

> *dance, you don't drink alcohol, you don't attend rock concerts . . . What do you do for fun?"*
>
> *Her answer was a great message for all Christians with conviction. She told him, "For fun I get up in the morning without feeling embarrassed, ashamed and guilty about what I did the night before." The young man had nothing more to say.*

It is true. That is fun! Come to think of it, there are many things in her life that are fun. She is now married to a fine Christian young man. They have a little girl and are building an outstanding Christian home together.

She is having fun every day not having to live with the affliction of deep scars and regrets from her past. It is fun getting all prettied up each afternoon to greet her husband after work, knowing he won't be stopping off at a local bar for a few drinks with the fellows. It is fun knowing that while he is away from her, his Christian values won't allow him to be unfaithful or flirt with other women. It is fun watching him hold his little girl on his lap with protecting, loving arms. It is fun knowing that her little girl will never see her father in a drunken stupor or experimenting with drugs. It is fun living with the assurance that their home will be led by a spiritual leader who will guide his family members to heaven.

The list of fun things for Christians is endless . . .What do you do for fun?

One young lady wrote this note, "My own personal struggle is not doing enough to show people that I am a Christian."

Remember that the decisions you make concerning your recreation will help others see that you are choosing to follow Christ. Your life and the lives of others will be blessed for it!

Remember the story of the rich young ruler in the Bible? He was not willing to give up all of his "stuff" and follow Christ. However, we are told in Luke 18:29, "Assuredly, I say to you, there is no one who has left house or parents or brothers or wife or children, for the sake of the kingdom of God, who shall not receive many times more in this present time, and in the age to come eternal life." Is that verse saying that we should all leave our families? Of course not! It is saying that when you give up things that you enjoy because you love the Lord, you will be blessed many times over! God knows your heart, and He will bless you for making the right choices concerning your recreation even if other people don't understand right now. When they see the strong person you will become because you have put the Lord first in your life, many of them will respect and admire you for the choices you have made.

Let Philippians 4:13 be the encouragement you need . . . . because you really can do all things through Christ who will strengthen you!

Questions
Chapter 6

1) Have you ever wondered how you were going to handle your commitment to sports and your commitment to God? How did that turn out for you? Have you made the right choice? How do you know?

2) How does the dictionary define recreation? How do we sometimes let our recreation control our lives? Do we often submit to the rules of our recreation gladly, but not to the Word of God? Why?

3) What does the word "glorify" mean? Why is it sometimes hard to glorify God in our recreation?

4) How will people know that you love the Lord if you constantly put your recreation before Him?

5) Read Hebrews 10:25 again. How would it be possible for you to forsake the assembly for your recreation?

6) Talk about some of the young people in the Bible who put God first in their lives even in very difficult circumstances.

7) God has given you the same characteristics he gave Timothy in 2 Timothy 1:7. What are those

characteristics? Does this mean that fear does not come from God?

8) Although Timothy was young, God expected him to be an example to the believers in six things. What were they? Do you think you are expected to do the same thing? Why or why not?

9) 1 Peter 3:4 tells us something that God prizes in women. What is it?

10) What does it mean when we try to rationalize something? Have you ever known that something was wrong but tried to rationalize that it would be O.K.? Maybe you can share this with the class.

11) Read Romans 8:31. What does this mean to you?

12) How can you do more to let others know that you are a Christian?

It's A Jungle Out There!
Or
"I'll be careful . . . ."

"See then that you walk circumspectly (carefully), not as fools but as wise, redeeming the time, because the days are evil. Therefore do not be unwise, but understand what the will of the Lord is."

Ephesians 4:15-17

Megan Meier was a thirteen-year old girl from Missouri with a My Space account. Her mother, Tina, monitored her daughter's account regularly. One day Megan was contacted by a young man named Josh Evans who asked to be put on her friends list. He had sent a picture and Megan showed his picture to her mother. Megan thought he was "hot" and her mother agreed that he was quite good looking. She agreed to let Megan add him as a friend. For six weeks, Josh and Megan communicated regularly on My Space. He told her that he had just moved from Florida and did not have a phone yet. Megan was happier than she had been in a long time. She had lost 20 pounds, she was getting her braces off soon, her birthday party was coming up and she had a very good looking boy interested in her!

And then one day, Josh sent a strange message. He said he didn't think he wanted to be her friend anymore because he had heard that Megan was not nice to her friends. She could not understand why he would say that. And then Megan began receiving messages saying that she was fat and that she was a slut. The last message her father read on her computer was, "the world would be a better place without you."

As Megan ran to her room after reading the messages, she bumped into her father in the hallway. He assured her that something was wrong with young people who hurt each other like that and that she was a very special young lady. Apparently that was not enough. Her dad then went downstairs into the kitchen and talked with Tina, Megan's mother, about the My Space account and how troubling it was sometimes.

"But I say to you, love your enemies, bless those who curse you, do good to those who hate you, and pray for those who spitefully use you and persecute you."
Matthew 5: 43-44

About twenty minutes later, Megan's mother, said she felt an odd chill and knew something was wrong. She called for Megan and ran upstairs to her room. Megan had hung herself in her bedroom closet. She was taken to the hospital but died the next day. Her parents were devastated.

This sad story does not end here. A few weeks later, a neighbor called Megan's parents and asked them to meet her at a counselor's office. They had no idea why. When they arrived, they were told by the neighbor that there never was a boy named Josh Evans. Josh had been made up by one of the mothers in the neighborhood who wanted to see what Megan was posting on the Internet about her daughter, once a friend of Megan's. She and her daughter, along with a co-worker, all pretending to be Josh Evans, kept up the communication with Megan. It turned out to be a very tragic joke.

How Can I Love My Enemies?

Cyberbullying is one of the reasons it is a jungle out there. Cyberbullying is when a child, preteen or teen is tormented, threatened, harassed, humiliated, lied about, embarrassed or hurtfully targeted by someone else using the Internet or text messaging.

In Megan's case, the bullying was done by a parent! You may believe that you know every person on your friends list when actually, you don't. Anyone can send a picture, make up a background and begin communication. It is important for you to understand that anyone can say anything about you. THAT DOES NOT MAKE IT TRUE. One thirteen-year old boy in Vermont committed suicide after being bullied online by peers who spread rumors that he was gay.

How can you avoid being a part of cyberbullying? For one thing, remember that Jesus Christ would never want us to hurt someone in this way. As a matter of fact, He was all about loving our enemies. He was all about blessing people who lie about you and doing good things for people who would like nothing more than to hurt you! That is not what the world teaches us, is it? The world would tell you that you have a "right" to get back at someone who has hurt you. People in this world, and many television programs, try to show you that "payback" is fun. Many would tell you that you didn't deserve to be treated like that!

Jesus tells us something completely different about dealing with those who would hurt us. Jesus says, "You have heard that it was said, 'You shall love your neighbor and hate your enemy.' But I say to you, love your enemies, bless those who curse you, do good to those who hate you, and pray for those who spitefully use you and persecute you" (Matthew 5: 43-44). Now why in this world would we want to do that? Does that make sense? Nobody we know does that; but our Father tells you and me to do that! Why?

Because we are his daughters, and we answer to Him. We should return good for evil so "that you may be sons (children) of your Father in heaven; for He makes His sun to rise on the evil and on the good, and sends rain on the just and on the unjust. For if you love those who love you, what reward have you? Do not even the tax collectors do the same? And if you greet your brethren only (or your friends only) what do you do more than others? Do not even the tax collectors do so?"

You need to understand that most people in the first century despised the tax collectors who often collected more taxes then they were supposed to in order to make themselves rich. Jesus was telling them that even the despised tax collectors love the people who love them. Just to love and be kind to those who are kind to you makes you no better than corrupt and dishonest people like the tax collectors.

Nobody's Perfect . . . Are They?

Jesus goes on to say, "Therefore you shall be perfect, just as your Father in heaven is perfect." The word "perfect" here means to be complete.

The word "perfect" is used the same way in 2 Corinthians13:1, Ephesians 4:13 and Colossians 1:28. The "perfect" Christian is not a person who never sins. She is a person who tries to be completely like Christ. Will we make mistakes? Sure we will, but the Bible tells us to "go on to perfection." In other words, keep trying. That will make us different from the world.

When I polled hundreds of girls about what advice they would give a young Christian, their advice was overwhelmingly "never, never, never give up!" In other words, no matter what happens, no matter how many times you get sidetracked, keep trying to be a complete Christian!

Jesus also tells us that people who are lied about and talked about unjustly will be blessed. In Matthew 5, He tells us : "Blessed are the meek," "Blessed are those who are persecuted for righteousness' sake" (just because you are trying to be good); "Blessed are you when they revile and persecute you (because you are trying to be different) and say all kinds of evil against you falsely for My name's sake" (because you are a Christian).

Bullying in any way or hurting another person for retaliation or for sport is totally against the nature of Christ. It should be totally against the conscience of a person who claims to love the Lord and who is trying to be like Christ. When our Lord had been beaten, lied about, spit upon, humiliated FOR NO REASON, He did not retaliate. He could have called thousands of angels to do His bidding. Instead, while history reports that some of the robbers and thieves had their tongues cut out by the Roman soldiers because they were cursing so violently . . . .our Lord, the Christ that we want to be like, said to His Father (the same Father we have), "Father, forgive them, for they don't know what they do" (Luke 23:34). He is our greatest example.

Think Before You Click!

If you ever receive a bullying message on the internet, do not respond. Stop and block all communication with that person. Tell a trusted adult, preferably a parent. Also, think about every communication you send. What if what you are sending was being sent about you or to you? How would it make you feel? Put yourself in the other person's position before you send it. THINK before you CLICK. Also, never give any personal information to anyone you meet online. That includes your first or last name, phone number (which can be used to track where you live), passwords, birth dates or years, school information or credit card information.

This Great Guy is a Robot!?

There is now a robot that has been invented who talks like a flirty stranger in many Internet chatrooms. According to Fox News, Internet security experts say that Russian programmers have created software known as CyberLover that can infiltrate dating sites and chatrooms and patiently seduce its victims. His main purpose is identity theft, and Internet experts say that the robot can make the acquaintance of between 10 and 20 people in half an hour. The report says that not a single girl has yet guessed that she is talking to a computer program. How romantic!

If you ever receive a bullying message on the internet, do not respond. Stop and block all communication with that person.

Here are some suggestions that can help you avoid a very bad situation. Please pay attention to them . . .

(1) Don't plan to meet anyone you don't already know and don't tell your schedule on the Internet.

(2) Don't tell anyone your plans for the day or for the week. Don't fill out any of those "fun" questionnaires that are forwarded to you no matter who they come from. Remember, everything in them can get forwarded and could end up in the hands of someone who would hurt you. More and more studies show that at least one out of every four young people get sexual solicitations online.

(3) Be very careful about posting pictures of yourself. These pictures often become a shopping mall for online predators. The best advice is not to post them at all, but if you must, don't post sexy ones or ones showing behavior you wouldn't want your mom, teacher, boss or potential college advisor to see.

There is even a site on Facebook on which young women (I really can't call them young ladies) post pictures of themselves when they are drunk. They are doing embarrassing and humiliating things. Many of them post their names and the colleges they attend even though anyone can take a look (including parents and future employers, not to mention perverted people).

One young lady took a drunken video of herself off of the Internet after CNN contacted her for an interview. She said it was then that she realized that anyone could see the video. She also said she was glad that her parents saw the video because it caused her to think a lot more about the jungle out there. She said that she worried that future employers would see the video. Her comment was, "I have no intentions of being wrapped around a toilet on the job."

More than once, our son, who is a youth minister, has had to show parents what their sons and daughters have posted on the Internet. In every case, it was because it could be potentially harmful to the young person and certainly not representative of a Christian. The more you talk on the Internet or IM about personal things, the more open you are to being bullied, disrespected, made fun of and ultimately hurt.

You and a parent or trusted adult might want to "Google" your name occasionally to see what information is out there about you. This could stop cyberbullying early. Most cyberbullying involes young people up to the age of about 14. After that, it tends to become sexual harassment or hacking attacks. Cyberbullying can be done on a person's blog, on a person's web site, started by internet polls, (ex. "Who's Hot and Who's Not?"), interactive gaming, sending porn and other junk email, and even impersonation (sometimes as a victim).

Why Do Teens Cyberbully Each Other?

Why do teens cyberbully each other? One article, entitled Parry's Guide to Cyberbullying says this, "When it comes to cyberbullying, young people are often motivated by anger, revenge or frustration. Sometimes they do it for entertainment or because they are bored and have too much time on their hands and too many tech toys available to them. Many do it for laughs or to get a reaction. Some do it by accident, and either send it to the wrong recipient or didn't think before they did something. The Power-Hungry do it to torment others and for their ego. Revenge of the Nerd may start out defending themselves from traditional bullying only to find that they enjoy being the tough guy or gal. Mean Girls do it to help bolster or remind people of their own social standing. And there are a few who think they are righting wrongs or standing up for others."

Another thing to remember is that along with this technology comes the "proof" of what was said, and who sent it. You may be confronted with the hard evidence of what you have written.

One important thing to remember is to get away from the computer for a while when something upsets you. Just take a "time out." Do something you enjoy doing. It may keep you from doing something you will regret later. Trust me.

Playing with Fire . . . You Will Get Burned!

Let me tell you about another young lady. She was eighteen years old, a secretary for an electric company by day and a business management student at night. This industrious young lady also had a website. On her website she was known as Zoey Zane. She appeared nude on her website and several "fan" sites of Zoey Zane had shown up on the Internet. She was seen leaving a bar one Friday evening with a man who is now being held by the police for her murder. Her body was found in the tall grass along Highway 54 in Kansas. Police wonder whether her web site with nude pictures of herself is the reason she was murdered. It may or may not be the reason she was murdered, but this young lady was definitely leading a life that had every possibility of ending tragically.

Solomon tells us in Proverbs 2 that, "Discretion will preserve you; understanding will keep you, to deliver you from the way of evil, from the man who speaks perverse things, from those who leave the paths of righteousness to walk in the ways of darkness; who rejoice in doing evil, and delight in the perversity of the wicked; whose ways are crooked, and who are devious in their paths."

How can you possibly be fleeing sexual immorality if you are flirting with it on the Internet?

We have discussed the word "discretion" in a previous chapter, but it is important to understand how important it is for you to be discreet in the jungle out there. It can keep you from harm. It can keep you away from people who rejoice in doing evil and who are perverse. And believe me, there are plenty of perverse people in this world. And that is not just because you live in America today with a World Wide Web. There have always been many perverse people in the world. The Bible gives us many examples of wicked, perverse people. (Think Jezebel, here!)

Before Noah built the ark, the Bible says that "the Lord saw that the wickedness of man was great in the earth, and that every intent of the thoughts of his heart was only evil continually" (Genesis 6:5).

But I'll Know if He Looks Dangerous . . .

I would like to tell you that you can recognize a wicked or perverse person by their appearance, but the truth is that you most likely will not. Child molesters, serial killers, drug dealers and sexually perverse people look, for the most part, just like us. Jeffrey Dahmer who killed, maimed and ate the body parts of some of his victims was actually a very neat, nice looking guy. Also, Ted Bundy, a well-known serial killer was considered very handsome by many women.

Just like living in the jungle . . . in this world you need to be smart, pay attention and run when you sense a predator near. You need to be confident and bold. God and the Bible will help you do that. Let the love of Christ, the Word of God and your love for Jesus be the ark that keeps you set apart from a world drowning in wickedness. Jesus died so that you could do that. You do not have to believe or buy into what this world is telling you and what the Internet and the media are selling you!

Are You Fleeing or Flirting?

The Bible tells us in 1 Corinthians 6 . . . "Flee sexual immorality. Every sin that a man does is outside the body, but he who commits sexual immorality sins against his own body." How can you possibly be fleeing sexual immorality if you are flirting with it on the Internet? Flirting with immorality on the Internet may seem safe because there is no one right in the room with you. But the fact is, you become a target of hundreds or thousands of predators instead of just one. And the person who loves and cares for you more than anyone else IS in the room with you. Our Father is not always with us to give us demerits when we make mistakes. That is an entirely wrong picture of God. God is there lovingly watching over you, ready to help you succeed at overcoming any temptation!

Pigtails and Porn...

A recent article called "Pigtails and Porn" by columnist Kathleen Parker reports that 42% of Internet users between that ages of 10 and 17 have viewed online pornography. The University of New Hampshire researchers found that two-thirds of those exposed to porn didn't want to see the images and did not seek them out. Most of these were ages 13 to 17, though a disturbing number were 10 to11 year olds. Researchers also found that unwanted pornography was flashed into homes on the screens despite the use of filtering and blocking software in more than half of the homes.

When I was studying last year for a Seminar on "Being Discreet", I googled the word "discretion." My screen was instantly filled with offers for a sexual, erotic afternoon or evening (for a fee, of course). These sites came up because the sites offering the fornication and adultery promised "discretion." In other words, no one would have to find out. The meaning of the word "discretion" I was searching for did not show up on the list of websites until I had filtered through a long list of pornographic sites.

Remember, too, that the owners, of Internet search engines often have an agenda. Their agenda will often be on the first pages they show you in your search. You may have to go through a long list of their preferences to find what you are looking for.

I know that in your Internet surfing and even in your research for school work, you may innocently run across pornography despite your and/or your parents efforts to keep it out of your home. It is not pretty and it is not realistic. Pornography is a sinful and addictive use of something that God has made special and beautiful in the marriage relationship. Studies have shown that viewing pornography can be addictive and psychologically and emotionally damaging. Many people are getting rich because they know that many first time viewers will return to their sites. Why do you think they will try every way in the world to get you to their site just once? Why do you think their ads often look innocent saying something like "Just for fun . . . click here." The fun turns out to be all kinds of lewd and sexually explicit pictures. You didn't mean to go there!

Let me show you something from the book of Psalms that applies here. Look at Psalm 1:1 . . . "Blessed is the man who walks not in the counsel of the ungodly, nor stands in the paths of sinners, nor sits in the seat of the scornful;." The passage goes on to say that this man will not prosper or do well. Do you see the progression here? At first this person just listened to the counsel of the ungodly. Then he stood with them. And finally, He sat down with them. He would have done well if he had not even walked in the counsel of the ungodly, much less sat down there! **Remember this...**

Sin Always Takes You Further Than You Intended To Go, Keeps You Longer Than You Intended To Stay And Costs You More Than You Intended To Pay . . .

This is a natural progression of sin and it is especially true of pornography. First there is a glimpse, perhaps even accidental. Next, the person decides just to "walk by" or glance at a few more pictures. And then, after only a short time, he or she is spending hours "sitting" and viewing pornography on the Internet. Sin always takes you further than you intended to go, keeps you longer than you intended to stay, and costs you more than you intended to pay. The people who make pornography available on the Internet are well aware of that. They are begging you to take a look, because statistics show that many who view pornography for the first time will eventually get caught in the trap!

Many good relationships have been destroyed and homes broken because someone decided to take another look. If you have a relationship with someone who views pornography, it cannot end well unless that person can give it up. There are many people unwilling to end their sick relationship to sexual perversion, no matter what the cost . . . including their relationship with you! Always steer very clear of anyone who is involved in pornography in any way.

A "Pharm" Party . . . Not in the Barnyard!

Another deadly thing that is happening in this jungle is that there are more young people abusing prescription drugs. Although marijuana use is down substantially according to a recent White House report, many teens are engaging in "pharm parties." And it is not a trip to Old McDonald's Farm for teenagers. The word "pharm" here comes from the word pharmaceuticals (prescription drugs). Painkilling drugs seem to be the pharmaceuticals of choice. The study says that teens are abusing prescription

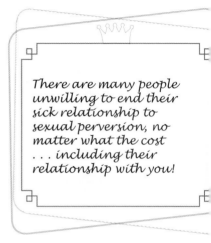

There are many people unwilling to end their sick relationship to sexual perversion, no matter what the cost . . . including their relationship with you!

drugs because they believe the drugs are safer than street drugs and easier to obtain. They can often get them over the Internet, from friends, or even in their household cabinets. Dr. Westley Clark, Director of the U.S. Center for Substance Abuse Treatment, said, "About 60% are getting their drugs from friends and family for free, while another 15% buy them from friends."

Some teens get to a party and find that a bowl has been filled with all kinds of prescription drugs. The partygoers pick a number and that is the position they will be in to pick a pill from the bowl. Most have no idea what they are taking or the side effects. It may be a costly momentary thrill and one you need to be well aware of. We are going to talk about parties in Chapter 8, but for now just be aware that this does go on and keep yourself safe in the jungle. Stay as far away from anything like this as you can.

I know that we live in a culture that prescribes a drug for just about anything. Drugs, however, will always be just a temporary fix that can become a lifetime addiction. I am sitting here right now with my leg in a cast and a bottle of pills sitting next to me labeled "May be habit forming." I had surgery on my foot last week and these are the pain pills that were given to me. Rather then even risk the chance of becoming addicted, I decided to try Extra Strength Tylenol just for a couple of days after the surgery, and they worked fine for me. You see, if I never take an addictive pain pill, I can never become addicted and the same goes for you!

Strong Mind . . . Strong Body
Weak Mind . . . Weak Body

There is also a strong correlation between substance abuse and mental health according to The National Survey on Drug Use and Health, (NSDUH). The survey points out that when young people turn to cigarettes, drugs or alcohol to try to deal with sadness or depression they are creating double jeopardy with their health and well-being. Turning to substance abuse is never the right answer. Turning to God and the truth of His Word is what will help keep you mentally strong.

Not Just an Alternate Lifestyle . . .

One other danger that I want us to see in the jungle is the danger of accepting homosexuality as a healthy lifestyle, when the Bible clearly teaches that it is not. Christians are often accused of hating homosexuals. That could not be further from the truth. Any person who loves the Lord and knows His Word knows that He died for homosexuals as sure as He died for you and me. He also died for murderers, thieves and liars. Jesus died to save us FROM these sins, not to save us IN them. Because of Him, we have the opportunity to live our lives free from sin, simply because we are forgiven when we repent (turn away from the sin).

Read 1 Corinthians 6: 9-11. Paul is talking to Christians who had been fornicators, idolaters, adulterers, homosexuals, thieves, drunkards and extortioners. Listen to what he says:

"And such were some of you. But you were washed, but you were sanctified, but you were justified in the name of the Lord Jesus and by the Spirit of God."

If we really do care about those who are practicing homosexuality, we will love them enough to kindly show them from the scriptures how they can be washed and justified to live in newness of life in Jesus Christ.

A front page article in USA Today in February, 2007, says that teens are "coming out" earlier to peers and family. My oldest granddaughter came home from kindergarten and asked me if Brittany Spears was gay. I asked her why she would think that. She said "I saw her kissing that other girl on T.V."

Do you really think that every girl you see kissing another girl on T.V., or in your school for that matter is a homosexual? I can tell you that many of them are not. Many times they are kissing each other for the attention it gets them from the boys and the girls! And some of them are trying to decide if they will choose to be homosexual. It is a choice. There are a few studies trying to link homosexuality to an inherited gene, but they have not been, and will not be, successful.

In the book, A Parent's Guide to Preventing Homosexuality, by Joseph and Linda Nicolosi, they share many case histories that point out why a person chooses homosexuality.

Let me share a small portion of one of those stories with you:

A twenty-five year old was in treatment for his un-wanted homosexuality. One day in sadness and anger he confronted his mother:

"Mom, you saw me play with Barbie dolls. You allowed me to use makeup and to fix my hair in front of a mirror for hours. My brothers never did any of this. Why didn't you stop me? What were you thinking?"

This mother should have encouraged her son's masculinity. She may have been listening to the mental health profession that is not telling us the truth about children's gender confusion. When I heard one little girl say that she was going to marry her life-sized Barbie doll at three years old, I immediately took the opportunity to tell her that girls don't marry girls. God made girls to marry boys!

Satan wants homosexuality to be portrayed as cute, fun, pleasant, natural and healthy when, in reality, it is none of the above. Homosexuality is a sin.

Charlene Cothran . . . Homosexuality is a choice!

Let me tell you about a lady named Charlene Cothran who emailed me for a book I have written for children about homosexuality. She was a lesbian for many years. She had a female lover named Venus. Venus was shot and killed by another lesbian, and Charlene Cothran started Venus Magazine in her memory several years ago. Venus Magazine was a successful magazine that encouraged and celebrated homosexuality, until recently. You see, Charlene Cothran started studying her Bible again and understood completely that her homosexuality was a choice. It is not genetic. If it was genetic, why are so many people able to change? She has often said that when she was living a homosexual lifestyle she did everything she could to try and make the Bible say that it was all right. She is now using her Venus Magazine to help others come out of the homosexual lifestyle. You won't see her story, or many other stories like hers on the evening news or read it in USA Today. They are just not that sensational to the world. Our adversary, the devil, does not want her story told.

Satan wants homosexuality to be portrayed as cute, fun, pleasant, natural and healthy when, in reality, it is none of the above. Homosexuality is a sin. There are many things in the Bible that are sinful. It is our responsibility not to take part in them. Are we to love people who willfully sin? Yes. We should love them enough to want to see them go to heaven. Certainly Jesus loved them that much and even gave His life on the cross for them. Are we to condone or take part in a sinful lifestyle? Absolutely not! As Christians, we are to "come out" of a sinful lifestyle and live daily in the presence of Christ, trying every day to keep away from Satan and from sin. Remember we read, "Resist the devil and He will flee from you" (James 4:7). Let the devil go on to easier prey in the jungle. You stay close to God, Jesus and the Bible.

Watch Out for the Lion!

Let's make sure that we are cautious and vigilant in this jungle of the world. Listen to what Peter tells young people in 1 Peter 5:8-9 "Be sober, be vigilant; because your adversary the devil walks about like a roaring lion, seeking whom he may devour. Resist him, steadfast in the faith, knowing that the same sufferings are experienced by your brotherhood in the world."

Our Father is looking for strong, young Christians in this world. He is counting on them to make this world a better place. You can be an Esther. Trust God. Resist the devil and he will flee from you.

"Draw near to God and He will draw near to you" (James 4:8).

Questions
Chapter 7

1) What is cyberbullying? Why is it so easy to do on the Internet?

2) Do you know people who make up names, send the wrong pictures and lie on the Internet? What is wrong with that? Is it any less wrong just because it is on the Internet? Why not?

3) Read Matthew 5: 43-45. How is this different than what many people in the world tell us?

4) Why did many people despise the tax collectors in Jesus' time?

5) Matthew 5:48 says, "Therefore you should be perfect, just as your Father in heaven is perfect." What does the word "perfect" mean here? According to this definition, can we try to be perfect?

6) What should you do if you ever receive a bullying message on the Internet?

7) Why is it so important to "THINK" before you "CLICK" ?

8) Why should you NEVER give personal information to someone you meet online?

9) What do you think motivates young people to take part in cyberbullying?

10) Why is it so important for you to be discreet when using the Internet? (See Proverbs 2: 11-18)

11) Will you always be able to recognize an evil or perverse person? Why or why not?

12) What can be the ark that keeps you from drowning in a world of wickedness?

13) Read 1 Corinthians 18:20. How does this apply to the jungle we are living in today? Do you think that the dangers of the jungle have always been there? Why or why not?

14) Do you think God is watching over you just to see if you make a mistake? Or do you think He is watching over you trying to help you succeed? Remember that He sent His only Son to die for you. What does that make you think about how much He loves you?

15) You may have a filter on your computer. Do you still need to be careful? Why? What does it mean to say that search engines often have an agenda? Why?

16) Why would anyone want to make you addicted to viewing pornography?

17) Read Psalm 1:1 again. How can that scene apply to pornography, alcohol, other drugs and sexuality? Explain.

18) What are some of the factors that might contribute to a person choosing to be a homosexual?

19) How can you personally draw near to God?

What About Parties?
Or
"Everyone's going!"

"Do not be deceived: Evil company corrupts good habits."
1 Corinthians 15: 33

I never thought of Haley as an evil companion. As a mater of fact, I thought she was pretty cool. She lived just down the street from me when I was in the ninth grade. Haley was an only child. It was obvious that she and her parents were determined that she should have every new gadget, the most fashionable clothes and the best circle of friends that money could buy. She was cute and she was a majorette. There was never anything that Haley did not have. Being from a family of five children, I was in awe of her. How could anyone be the center of her parents' world and their checkbook? Talk about a princess!

If Haley wanted something, it was the goal of her two doting parents to make sure that she had it. Usually, I was not in Haley's circle of friends. But at the beginning of ninth grade, Haley was having a party. I guess since I had moved on to her block (we practically had the same address!), she felt the need to invite me. I was thrilled! I was going to get to go to Haley's house with all of the other "in" girls. My parents had no idea how big this was to me. As a matter of fact, I am not sure anyone did. This meant I might have arrived!

For two weeks, I thought about what I would wear that would even be comfortable around Haley and her friends. No doubt every one of them would be wearing the best of everything. As far as clothes, I was sure I didn't have the "best" of anything!

The monumental night came. I had about five houses to pass as I walked to Haley's house. It seemed like a long way. I wanted to do everything right. I wanted her parents to like me. I wanted her friends to like me. I wanted to be a part of her group and tonight was my chance!

In the early evening, I remember having a pretty good time. I was not an insider but at least no one was rude to me. . . until later. You see, after about 9:30, Haley's parents vanished. They left us all downstairs and I never saw them again that night. However, all of the guests seemed in favor of playing "Spin the Bottle." I am sure that sounds archaic to you, but I was never in favor of kissing someone just because the spinning bottle landed on him. If I was going to kiss someone, it would be WHO I wanted to kiss, WHEN I wanted to kiss and IF I wanted to kiss. I remember sitting on the steps and watching boys and girls "choose" each other by the luck of the bottle. They could kiss in front of everyone or go into a downstairs closet. It seemed ridiculous to me. I remember being called a "prude," a "spoilsport" and "frigid." It ended up being a very unpleasant evening, and I went home much earlier than the others. I was sure I would never be invited to another one of their parties, and I was pretty sure I didn't care. That was the beginning of the end for me as far as being a part of the elite "girl's club" at school for the next four years.

God knows your heart and your motives, and He also knows that there are times when you need help with them.

Do You Think Jesus Was An Outsider?

There will be times when the choices you make will make you feel totally out of it, and it is hard to be an outsider . . . however, your choices can also give you a great sense of freedom. I wonder if Jesus felt like an outsider most of His life? I am pretty sure He did!

Many times during my high school years, I realized that most of the girls in my class had gotten into trouble at some time or another because of partying over the weekend. Because of my choices, I had not been invited to most of the drinking and drug parties, but I sure saw and read about the results of those supposedly good times!

I saw classmates involved in drunken driving accidents. I saw couples go from having great, fun relationships to having sex every weekend and then deciding they really didn't like each other so much after all! It seemed like after the sex became so important, the relationship was reduced to when and where. I saw classmates who had been date raped by a "friend."

Several of my classmates over the next four years were arrested for being minors in possession of alcohol. Most of the time it was either at a party, at a club or after a party. My high school class was notorious for how hard it could party.

I even had friends whose parents decided that they would supply the booze at their house so that their child would not be driving drunk after a party. In the years since then, their "enlightened" attitude has most often resulted in drunk driving charges at a later age for their children and several lifelong battles with alcoholism.

When you decide to opt out of partying, there might be times when you have to convince your parents that you are not depressed or suicidal, but just choosing to be alone. Believe me, God knows and understands. He will help you with your convictions. God knows your heart and your motives, and He also knows that there are times when you need help with them.

Lord, Please Help My Unbelief!

There is an interesting story in the New Testament about a father who brought his son to Jesus to have a mute spirit cast out of him. Jesus told the dad that if he could just believe, then all things were possible to the person who believes. Guess what? The father, right then and there, said with tears in his eyes, "Lord, I believe; help my unbelief" (Mark 9:24).

As a young lady, you are probably going to want to believe in God. You are probably going to want to do the right thing. You are probably even going to try to put Christ first in your life, but there are going to be times when you feel just like this father. "Lord, help my unbelief! Lord, I know you are there, you know my struggles . . .help me!"

It is not always just at a party that we find ourselves in an uncomfortable situation that we do not intend to get into. I remember in eighth grade deciding to join the Girl Scouts. I thought maybe I would fit in with that group. I was pretty smart, I liked the outdoors and joining the Girl Scouts seemed like a really wholesome thing to do. I enjoyed the meetings at the girls' houses and working on projects together . . . for about two months. And then came our first camp out. I was even excited about that. I was particularly interested in making s'mores around the campfire! All of it was fun until we were told to go to our tents for the night. Guess what the girls in my tent voted to do? Play strip poker! Guess who was the only person who did not vote to play strip poker and who sat in the corner of the tent out of the way most of the night? Also, guess who never went back to another Girl Scout meeting? I liked to have fun as much as the next person, but this was not my idea of fun!

People Know Who You Are by the Choices You Make

Our choices make us who we are. Thankfully, I was not always a complete wallflower. I dated a boy from another school during the tenth, eleventh and twelfth grades (More about that in Chapter 9). That gave me the freedom to be just friends with many of the young men in my own class. They knew I would not party with them or do anything I would regret. They knew that I was not dateable to them so we could easily just be friends. That took a lot of pressure off of my relationships with guys. I had lots of guy friends.

Remember what we said about friendship? All good relationships begin with friendship, including our relationships with guys. A relationship built on "love at first sight" can rarely endure the changes and the trials and tribulations of life like a relationship built on friendship.

I was editor of my high school newspaper and stayed very busy with that. I never attended a drinking or drug party. Why? Because I had let my standards be known early. Was I tempted sometimes? Of course. But being tempted is not the sin. I sat home many nights (even on the night of my graduation party) because I chose not to put myself in compromising situations that I might not be able to handle.

Do you know one of the best things that resulted from the choices I had made as a teenager? My parents trusted me. After the tenth grade, they let me make most of my own decisions about where to go and with whom. I still could not have my own car (I knew we couldn't afford that) and I was expected to be home at a decent hour, but my parents gave me great freedom after they realized the choices I was making. It kept a lot of tension out of our relationship.

The biggest problem with parties is that they almost always involve drinking.

Because I was not involved in their partying on weekends, I could listen to my classmates when they were hurting and help them deal with relationships gone sour. I ALWAYS, ALWAYS tried to keep my mouth shut about the things I knew about them unless it was a matter of life and death.

You can and should do the same thing. It will save you a lot of hassle and confusion in high school.

Alcohol Short Circuits the Brain!

The biggest problem with parties is that they almost always involve drinking. The United States Surgeon General recently reported that Americans need a wake-up call about the widespread use of alcohol by millions of underage drinkers. He described alcohol as the drug of choice for teenagers. He went on to say, "Alcohol remains the most heavily abused substance by America's youth. We must change the cultural attitudes toward drinking in America. We can no longer ignore what alcohol is doing to our children."

He urged more research on teen drinking and its relationship to mental and physical development. New research indicates that alcohol may harm the development of a teenager's brain. He also said that, "Too many Americans consider underage drinking a rite of passage to adulthood. Research shows that young people who start drinking before the age of 15 are five times more likely to have life-long alcohol problems." Remember this . . . not a single person who never took one drink of alcohol ever became an alcoholic!

The Bible tells us a lot about the effects of alcohol and why we should avoid drunkenness. Many tragic stories are a result of not listening to God's Word on this subject. In the Book of Proverbs, alcoholic wine is referred to as a mocker and a deceiver that leads to violence (20:21), sorrow (23:29-30), immorality (23:33), insecurity (23:34), insensibility (23:35); and is even compared to a poisonous snake (23:32)!

It's Hard to Be Different!

Let me share a story with you from the life of a young woman whom I admire very much. At one point in her life, she was just tired of being different. She said that she had kept her conviction about drinking at parties all through her high school years. She was from a faithful Christian family and during high school she saw many of the young people from Christian homes compromising their beliefs. There was big party brewing during the spring of her senior year. She wanted so badly to go! Her dad was withholding his permission and she was furious. He asked her the classic parent question, "If all of your friends were jumping off a bridge, would you?" She immediately answered, "Yes!"

We all feel like that sometime, don't we? Remember how hard it feels to be totally out of it?

Her dad relented and let her go. She decided that it couldn't hurt just to open a can of beer and carry it around. What could be wrong with that? She was tired of being different.

Thankfully, her Dad never heard that she had been drinking (which she actually had not, but how hard would it have been to convince him of that?). Now it was getting close to graduation and she was relieved that she could put that party behind her.

When their high school yearbooks came out everyone was busy getting them signed. One afternoon, as she was reading through her annual, one young man had written, "We are glad that you finally decided to be like the rest of us!" She was hurt, sad and sorry. Had she really become a drinker? No. Had she wanted to look like it? Yes. It had been a bad choice. You never know how your choices are going to affect the lives of others and their perception of you.

What's Up with Partying in College?

After high school and during the first few months of college, this party thing got a little blurred for me. I was a member of a sorority and I was a little sister to a fraternity. There were lots of parties every weekend and there was hardly anyone at Tennessee Tech who knew or cared how I felt about drinking and drugs. There were students at Tennessee Tech from ages 16 to 50 and there were even quite a few partying professors! This was new ground for me. I was seventeen years old.

When I began dating at Tech, there were parties every weekend and I began dating a lot of different guys. After a few months, it was pretty well known in the fraternity circles that I didn't drink or sleep around. (Word traveled fast among those frat brothers!) However, they still invited me to parties and wanted me to be a little sister to the fraternity.

Many of these fraternity parties were keg parties. I saw many sweet young ladies lose all of their inhibitions (and usually their virginity) after they were loaded up with alcohol. Remember, I was not a Christian at this time in my life and did not understand that God warns us about the things that go on at parties. Read Galatians 5:19-21. It is obvious that the uncleanness, lewdness, drunkenness and revelries (dancing) talked about as being works of the flesh are all a part of the partying scene. A young lady who loves the Lord will avoid putting herself in the middle of such ungodliness.

Dancing is Just Dancing, Right?

Let me share something with you that happened at one of these parties. Although I did not drink, I did dance. As a matter of fact, I enjoyed dancing and often argued that I didn't see anything lewd about it. I sure could not help it if some guy with a dirty mind did.

At this particular fraternity party, there was an older guy who had served in Vietnam. Older to me was about 24 years old. All of the fraternity brothers loved him and respected that he had been in the war. They were actually quite proud of him.

On this evening, I was dancing with my date and just having a good time. During one of the songs, I noticed that my date and I were the only two people left on the dance floor and everyone else was watching us. Now this was totally unusual because, frankly, I was not that GREAT of a dancer, and neither was he. All at once, I felt something or someone brush up behind me. I turned to find this older fraternity brother dancing as close up to me as he could without touching me with his pants pulled down. I was embarrassed and furious. And to make matters worse, his fraternity brothers took up for him by saying, "He's drunk. He doesn't realize what he is doing."

Needless to say, I decided that night that I would not be dancing at parties anymore. I decided that, in a way, I could control what someone was thinking . . . at least about me!

Just recently, Fox News ran a story about "freaking" being banned at a school in Argyle, Texas. Here is what the principal said:

"Freaking is not just shaking your booty." he said. "This is pelvis-to-pelvis physical contact in private areas and then moving around. I have no doubt that the current cleavage-baring dress styles combined with sexually charged dancing could lead to an unsafe environment for students." Do you think?

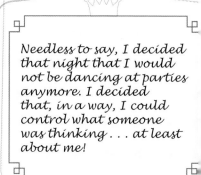

Needless to say, I decided that night that I would not be dancing at parties anymore. I decided that, in a way, I could control what someone was thinking . . . at least about me!

Many schools are following suit and banning the hip-hop inspired dancing. Dancing seems to be a socially legitimate excuse for many young ladies to flaunt their sexuality and practice the works of the flesh. Although it may be socially acceptable, a young lady who is glorifying God in her life will not find it spiritually acceptable.

The Deadly Unofficial Graduation Party . . .

Does the name Natalie Holloway mean anything to you? She was a high school graduate from Alabama having the unofficial graduation party of her life in Aruba when she went missing. No one knows what happened to Natalie Holloway. Do you know what? When it was happening, I doubt if she knew either. She was probably stoned, drugged or passed out at the time. Her own classmates in a *Vanity Fair* article said that she had been drinking all day long the day before her disappearance. The investigators indicated that the police have evidence that shows that to be true. There is also evidence that Natalie Holloway had drugs, but not necessarily that she was taking them. There are many theories about her death and one of them that keeps resurfacing is that Natalie Holloway did not die of a violent crime, but of alcohol poisoning.

Her dad went to Aruba to visit the bar where Natalie was last seen leaving in a car with three young men. He was told by the Aruban authorities, "She might turn up there, but watch your drink, 'Because people put stuff in it'" according to Fox News in 2006.

When I was in college many years ago, I was not afraid to walk around at a party with a soft drink in my hand. I could have even set it down for a minute and never worried that someone would put something tasteless and colorless in it that would make me incapable of acting on my convictions.

Today you cannot and must not leave an open container unattended at any time. I had a youth worker tell me last summer that two of her young ladies had been date raped because of setting down a soft drink at a party and picking it up again! Let me tell you again . . . when alcohol or drugs are introduced, you become someone you might not recognize the next day. You often become totally oblivious to your choices. Why in the world do you think that drugs and alcohol are such an important part of a party? Why do you think young men like for young ladies to drink?

The classmates of one young lady, who is still missing, have reported that she let the young man who is the prime suspect in her disapearance drink alcohol from her naval as she lay on top of the bar. Is it any wonder that many guys like for girls to drink? If a young man is encouraging you to drink, it is because of what is in it for him. He does not really care about you.

Partying and Date Rape . . .

It is not surprising that the highest incidence of date rape with an acquaintance occurs in grade twelve and during the freshman year of college. It is during this time that a young person parties the most!

It is important for you to have a good reputation. If you have made good choices you will not be seen as an easy prey. Unfortunately there are plenty of other girls who like to drink and are no longer virgins and most young men would be more likely to target one of them. Occasionally there is a young man who will pursue you just to see if he can be your first. You would be nothing but a conquest for him. Save that conquest for the person whom you choose to marry and not for someone just because you ended up at a party with him!

Just yesterday a young woman attempted to sell her four year old son to help pay for her wedding dress. She offered her son to a retailer for $200 to cover the balance of a bill for the dress. How could any mother do this? The prosecutor requested that this young woman go to prison. He said her "out-of-control behavior" was fueled by alcoholism. The book of Proverbs tells us that people become out-of-control when they consume alcohol.

Becoming "Fit" for The Kingdom

Let me share with you the struggle that one young lady described to me:

"As a teenager, I struggle with doing what's right and living a righteous life. Instead of sticking out as a Christian, sometimes I give in to the world of being a teenager and having fun even though I want to be a good Christian."

Another young lady put it this way, "My own personal struggle is sitting back and doing what God says instead of participating in certain activities."

And yet another young lady states, "My own personal struggle is keeping away from things that will make me fit in or be fun even though I know it is wrong,"

Other advice from the girls that I surveyed was, "Don't put yourself in a bad situation, and don't let the world pull you into what it thinks is right when we know it is wrong."

God did not put us here to "fit in" but to become "fit" for the kingdom of heaven. There is so much joy in knowing that you are living your life to do that. God knows your struggles. He will strengthen you. Memorize Philippians 4:13 which says, "I can do all things through Christ who strengthens me." Keep this verse close to your heart.

Questions
Chapter 8

1) How can the choices you make sometimes make you an outsider? Has this ever happened to you? Even though it might not feel so great at the time, how can being an outsider give you a sense of freedom?

2) Why do you think Jesus might have felt like an outsider most of His life?

3) Do your parents understand that there are times that you just want to be alone? How can you assure them that it's okay?

4) Read Mark 9:24 again. Will God help your unbelief? How do you think He does that?

5) How can the choices you make keep a lot of tension out of your relationship with your parents?

6) What is the drug of choice for teenagers? Why?

7) How does alcohol affect your mental and physical development?

8) Why is it good for you to remember that not a single person who never took one drink of alcohol ever became an alcoholic?

9) What do we learn in Proverbs about the results of drinking?

10) How are the choices you are making right now going to affect what people think about you? Should your reputation be important to you? Why?

11) What does alcohol do to your inhibitions (those things that you really think that you should not do)?

12) Why must you never leave an open container of something you are drinking alone for a second?

13) Why would men (young or old) encourage young ladies to drink?

14) Discuss reasons why the incidence of date rape is highest during the senior year of high school and the freshman year of college?

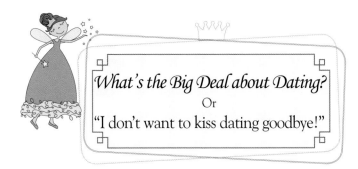

What's the Big Deal about Dating?
Or
"I don't want to kiss dating goodbye!"

"For you were bought with a price; therefore glorify God in your body and in your spirit, which are God's."

1 Corinthians 6: 20

I want to say at the outset of this chapter that I still believe dating is an acceptable thing for a strong Christian young lady to do. On the other hand, I would question the practice of dating for any young lady who is not dedicated to trying to live like Christ. That young lady is going to have a much more confusing and turbulent experience during her teenage years.

If you are going to glorify God in your body and in your spirit, then you must decide how you are going to behave on a date long before you ever have one. Glorifying God in your spirit means loving Him and making decisions that please Him.

Do you remember when Daniel was a young man and he was brought to the king's palace? In Daniel:1, we learn that Daniel had "no blemish, was good-looking, gifted in all wisdom, possessed knowledge and was quick to understand." (Sounds like someone we would like to date, doesn't it?)

When Daniel was offered the king's delicacies and the wine which the king himself drank, the Bible tells us that Daniel had already (before he was offered the food and drink) "purposed in his heart that he would not defile himself with the portion of the king's delicacies, nor with the wine which he drank" (Daniel 1:8).

This is how a Christian young lady should approach dating. She has already purposed (decided) in her heart and in her prayers how she is going to act on a date.

What is Dating . . . Actually?

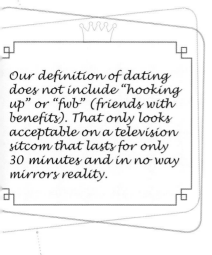

Our definition of dating does not include "hooking up" or "fwb" (friends with benefits). That only looks acceptable on a television sitcom that lasts for only 30 minutes and in no way mirrors reality.

For our definition of dating, let me share with you the process I am talking about. Girl meets boy. They talk casually. The two enjoy being in each other's company. The boy asks the young lady to go out on a date with him. However, there are some things that need to happen in the meantime. I personally might have invited him over to my house just so my parents could have met him before asking them if they would let me go out in a car with him. You see, I never did see them hand over their car keys to a stranger and let that stranger take their cars out for a spin. I doubted if they were going to let their daughter go out in a car with a young man whom they knew nothing about. I planned for them to say yes, so I always made sure that my parents knew a lot about my future dating prospect (and his parents, if possible).

Our definition of dating does not include "hooking up" or "fwb" (friends with benefits). That only looks acceptable on a television sitcom that lasts for only 30 minutes and in no way mirrors reality. The results of these two situations are devastating and damaging, and in no way can they really be defined as a relationship. You are kidding yourself if you think that they are. If you understand that real life (and sex) are not like the movies and television sitcoms you are well on your way to being a young lady who can date with integrity.

The Bible defines "hooking up" and "fwb" as fornication and sexual immorality (Ephesians 5:5; Hebrews 13:4). In the book, Dateable, by Justin Lookadoo and Hayley DiMarco, Justin says, "Easy girls are not keepers. They are just a temporary fix until the right one comes along. . . . an easy girl may get a short-lived rush that will leave her alone and all used up."

Our definition of dating is the process by which we become the right girl (who has put the Lord first in her life) while we wait for the right guy!

My first exclusive relationship was in ninth grade. Since David could not drive yet, my parents would let him come to my house on Saturdays and stay until late in the evening. He ate meals with us, played with my brothers and kissed me goodnight at the front door in my parents' living room and then walked four miles home. It was a wholesome relationship that lasted through the ninth grade.

That was until we moved and I met Kevin. Kevin was hot. He was a lifeguard at the local swimming pool, over six feet tall, intelligent, and he had great posture! (I loved for a guy to stand up straight!) Kevin went to a different school. We were introduced by a mutual friend. Kevin was a really good athlete and a member of the church of Christ (which I knew very little about at the time). Kevin started coming by my house in the evenings after the swimming pool closed. We sat on the porch for hours talking and found that we really liked each other.

Nobody Said Breaking Up Wasn't Hard To Do . . .

In the meantime, I knew that I had to break up with David. Now some people say that this is a reason not to date. They say that breaking up is too hard and that usually someone gets hurt. I am going to suggest to you that it is a part of dating that you have to be willing to chance if you are going to date different people.

One young lady, Linda, wrote to me, "I am getting out of a bad relationship with a boy I liked a lot. I'm trusting that God will send me a good godly guy and I am putting my trust in God."

How much better for her to get out of the relationship now and trust the Lord, than to continue in the relationship because she doesn't want anyone to be hurt.

Sometimes you may be the one getting hurt, or you may be the one who has to hurt someone else. But I have to emphasize this . . . make sure that you have done nothing to be ashamed of. Make sure that the other person still respects you because you have not given yourself to him sexually. This is why you must purpose in your heart that dating a person does not mean that you owe him anything! In this case, I found out something about David that I did not know. It was something that made me see that he was not someone I would want to marry. When I told David at school that I wanted to break up, he became furious and rammed his hand through a locker! I was so glad that I told him at school because it was so public. I had never experienced David's temper before and I was so thankful that I saw it then. I realized right then that he was not a future marriage prospect.

Look for the Red Flags...
The Time to Get a Divorce!

Listen to me, young ladies. A bad temper is a red flag. Let me share a story with you:

A young lady who had been married less than a year, went to talk with her preacher. She said she was considering getting a divorce. The preacher asked her why. She said that her husband would not come to worship with her. The preacher then asked her if her husband came to worship with her before they got married. She answered, "Well, he always said he wanted to, but that his parents wouldn't let him."

Young ladies, this is a red flag! Don't think for one minute that many young men will not out right lie to you. They will. I dated a great guy that I really liked, but his car always smelled like smoke. I lived in a house full of smoke and I detested it. Every time I questioned him about his smoking, he always said that the smoke smell was from the cigarettes of his friends. It is a funny thing that after we quit dating, I saw him smoking many times!

Anyway, the young lady then went on to tell her preacher that her husband drank. The preacher was so disappointed and said, "Did he drink before you got married?"

The young lady answered, "Yes. But he told me he would stop after we were married." (Another red flag!)

The preacher explained to her that those were not scriptural reasons for getting a divorce. And then she really stunned him by blurting out, "But he hits me!"

The preacher looked at her sadly now. "Did he hit you any time before you were married?"

"Well, no," the young lady answered, "but he did raise his hand to me several times like he was going to."

The preacher was hurting with her by this time. He answered, "Honey, the time for you to get a divorce was before you ever married that young man!"

Dating is about learning about someone else and learning about yourself. You actually teach people how to treat you by how you react to them, by how you react to drinking, by how you react to the latest dirty joke, by how you react to sexual advances, by how you react to your family and a host of other things. You also get to see how the person you are considering dating reacts to these same situations.

Let me share some comments with you from Christian young ladies who have dated in the past and who are happily married today.

"Do not date someone who wants to control you" . . . Suzy

"Don't change yourself for him. Always remember to be yourself" . . . Brittany.

"There is time when you need your own space and he needs his. You both need to keep your individuality." . . . Melanie

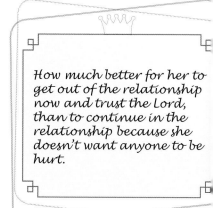

How much better for her to get out of the relationship now and trust the Lord, than to continue in the relationship because she doesn't want anyone to be hurt.

"Be mindful of where you first come in contact with your date. This can tell a lot about the type of person he is. Also, past behavior is the best indicator of future behavior. If he has done something questionable, violent or irresponsible with other girls, then he will do it with you." . . . Angie

"Dating is a wonderful thing but take your time, get to know the person" . . . .Allison

"Know and learn all you can about a young man before you make the decision to go alone on a date with him" . . . Barbara

"Find out and see what his family is like. The young man will more than likely have the same habits and be-liefs that his family has." . . . .Mary

"I would say to take a deep look at how a young man talks about and treats his mother. Many young men will treat his future wife like he treats his mother" . . .Fay

He Might Make a Better Actor than Husband . . .

Remember, anyone can put on a good act for a while. It takes time to see someone in different situations. I often watched to see how my dates treated waiters and wait-resses. Was he kind to them? Was he rude to them? This gives you a pretty good indication of how he really treats people. If you are the one he is dating at the moment, he will be much nicer to you. You will see the real person in how he talks about and treats others.

And speaking of waiters and waitresses . . . you should expect your date to pay for the date. Does that sound old fashioned to you? Well, the truth is that it is not old fashioned but it is an indicator of how much he values you. Believe me, he pays for everything else that's important to him. If a date with you is no more important than purchasing the latest CD, then he doesn't think much of you!

One of the things that drew me to my husband was that he believed it was his responsibility to take care of me, even when we were dating. I was taught to be an inde-pendent and capable young lady. But just having a young man who thought enough of me to plan a date instead of always saying, "What do you want to do?" was refreshing to me. After I said yes to a date, Stan would plan some-thing fun for us to do. That made me feel like he really was interested in me and that I was worth the effort. It didn't have to be expensive every time. Even though ev-ery now and then a nice dinner and a movie were a great treat, there were many times when both of us tried to sug-gest things to do that did not cost a lot of money.

We were both in college when we met, so sometimes we just sat in the swing in front of my dorm or went for a root beer float at the local Dairy Queen. Notice this: even though we were both in college, I expected him to pay. It was very good practice for the time several years later when I was home raising our three children and he was out earning a living for us. It is refreshing to find a young man who still believes that he is to be the breadwinner because his wife might like to be a stay home mom someday! Paying for a date is just the beginning of real manhood . . . look for someone who believes paying for the date is his responsibility and appreciate that he thinks enough of you to do that.

One young lady wrote: "My own personal struggle is that I have a problem with guys. I am scared that I'll be pressured into something I know is wrong."

Let me repeat here: You do not owe a young man anything because he took you out on a date. Do not ever feel pressured. If this is your attitude then you have not already purposed in your heart that you will obey God and you are not ready to date yet. If you want to do something nice for a young man who has been sweet to you . . . .bake him cookies! I guarantee you he will enjoy them.

Dating and Sex Are Not the Same Thing

When Kevin and I began dating in high school, we had a very good relationship and mutual respect for one another. We went to different schools, so that pretty much limited our dating to Saturday nights. Over the next couple of years, we double dated a couple of times with his best friend and his girlfriend. They were always in the backseat and I could tell that making out was a big part of their relationship. I was uncomfortable and after a couple of times, we never double dated again. Unfortunately, Kevin's best friend graduated as an expectant father and his girlfriend dropped out of high school.

My son recently told me about going to a local baseball game. The star pitcher was an eighth grader. This eighth grade boy had two girls sitting in the stands watching him play. Each had a baby who would call him daddy. These girls believed a lie. Every girl thinks that she is better than the last girlfriend. Every girl wants to believe that he likes (or loves?) her more.

After I had been at college a while, I realized that Kevin and I were not going to continue just dating each other. It had been a great situation for high school but I began to see things that disturbed me. For one thing, his parents had spoiled him and he thought the world was going to do the same thing. He had been handed everything and he did not have much of a work ethic. And one more important thing . . . it took him longer to get ready to go somewhere than it did me! Somehow, this did not bode well for me for a marriage partner.

You do not owe a young man anything because he took you out on a date. Do not ever feel pressured. If this is your attitude then you have not already purposed in your heart that you will obey God and you are not ready to date yet.

Also, his parents were always commenting to me, "Sheila, why don't you be baptized and then you and Kevin can get married." I thought this was odd, especially because no one asked to study the Bible with me. Why would I want to be baptized just so I could marry Kevin? Many times when we were driving back to college he would say, "Let's just go get married."

Was I tempted? Of course. I had dated him three years and I really was into the guy. But I reminded myself of those red flags.

Your Friends May See Something You Don't . . . or Won't!

By this time, my girlfriends were telling me that he was not exclusive when I was away at college. Of course, I did not believe them. I wasn't sure I wanted to believe them. Then I came home one weekend unexpectedly and saw him out with someone else. Was I furious? Of course. Was I hurt? Of course. Did I get a good dose of reality? Yes. That was the last red flag.

The next time Kevin called I told him to forget about us. He gave me the usual lines about why he happened to be out with her, but I was ready to move on. Now this is important . . . after three years I could move on with a clear conscience. I didn't owe him anything. He didn't own any part of me. We dated. That's all! End of story.

Did I ever think of him again? Yes. I suppose he thought a lot about me, too. For the most part, our memories of each other were very good. We had no regrets. We did not carry a lot of unhealthy physical or emotional baggage away from our relationship. We simply dated in high school and learned a lot about ourselves and relationships in the process.

Then came dating in college. I guess I always knew that Kevin was not the one I would marry, because I chose to go to a college that had a boy to girl ratio of seven to one. Seven boys for every girl! I knew I was not interested in being an engineer, but this school looked interesting to me!

Now What's so Great about the BMOC?

I had been at college a few months when one of the BMOC (Big Men on Campus) asked me for a date. We will call him Chase. He was about four years older than me and very well known and liked on campus. Needless to say, I was flattered. We dated a few times and he was very sweet to me. Then I began hearing things about him. I heard that he was a big drinker. Funny, he never took a drink with me. I heard that he cursed, but I never actually heard him curse. I heard that he used girls and then walked away. I did not intend to let myself be used by him.

One weekend he had asked me to go to meet his parents. This is the ultimate compliment. When a boy asks a girl to meet his parents, we start thinking house, home, husband and babies. They are thinking a weekend at home with a girl they can at least show to their parents!

After his parents went to bed that evening, Chase and I sat on the couch. He put his arm around me and began lowering his hand to my chest. I simply lifted his hand and put it back on my shoulder. He snapped, "I was not going to touch your boob!"

And he wasn't. I had already purposed in my heart that no one was going to touch me that way. We were dating, not married. When I got back to the dorm that weekend, I knew that was my last date with Chase.

Now listen to me. This is big! When your friends tell you things that you do not want to believe about a guy, you had better pay attention. They are your friends. They are not out to get you! They may very well see and notice things that you either do not see or know, or that you do not want to see and know. Will you want to listen to them? Probably not. Pay attention anyway.

A few weeks later this same BMOC started dating another young lady in my dorm. How ironic is this? Her name was Sheila. She obviously fell head over heels for him and just knew that he loved her more than the last girl he dated. That Sheila ended up pregnant and the BMOC joined the army to get away from any responsibility he might have had in the unfortunate event.

The Pregnant Teenager Has Three Choices . . .

When a teenager in our country gets pregnant she has three choices. She can parent the baby (a lifelong commitment); she can abort the baby (murder the child according to the Bible, Proverbs 6:17); or place the child up for adoption. Before a girl gets pregnant . . . she has a wonderful choice. That choice is not to have sex. In making that choice, her future is open to so many more options and possibilities without all of the physical and emotional consequences of pregnancy and premarital sex. Studies show that only 20 to 30 percent of teen fathers marry their baby's mother. Pregnancy is not a reason to get married. A baby will not hold a marriage together. If anything, it is added stress and commitment. A marriage based on a pregnancy is on very shaky ground.

Dating is Just Dating

Dating is dating. It is nothing more, nothing less. You determine (purpose in your heart) how you are going to handle dating. One young lady told me, "But I can't help it. I always give in."

What she told me is not true. She can help it. How she handles herself on a date is her choice. She can trust God, rely on his Word for guidance and know how she is going to behave on a date before she ever gets into that situation. Any other attitude toward dating will not glorify

God and any young lady who does not have that attitude should not be dating. The prince of this world (Satan) is just waiting for that young lady to start dating. And so are a lot of young men who are just looking to have a good time and see how many conquests they can make.

Sex and dating are not the same thing. Dating is an opportunity to find the person with whom you want to build a lifelong relationship. Sex is only one aspect of a relationship and is far less important than commitment to the other person no matter what. The emotional price is much too high when a girl equates dating with sex or believes that sex has to be a part of the dating relationship. Our Creator knows us best and He knows our desires and our needs. That is why He has reserved sex only for the marriage union. In marriage, sex is beautiful and fulfilling. Outside of the marriage relationship sex creates emotional and physical pain. God loves us and wants to protect us from that.

Remember that God created you in His image. You are a beautiful, worthy young woman. You are God's property. Your body belongs to God. You deserve to be honored, cherished and respected. Any young man who truly cares more about you than he does about himself will treat you that way. And if he doesn't . . . you would not want him for your lifelong companion.

What about Interracial Dating?

When I talk about dating with a group of girls, I always get a question about interracial dating. Some people use scriptures in the Old Testament to try and prohibit interracial dating and marriage. The Hebrews in the Old

Testament were warned against marrying Gentiles more out of keeping believers from marrying nonbelievers than because of race. Solomon is an example of someone who married women of different faiths who worshipped false gods. He had been warned in 1 Kings 11: 2 "Surely they will turn away your heart after their gods." The Bible says that Solomon "clung to these women in love."

You will eventually marry someone you date. Dating provides an opportunity to build good character, strengthen your faith, learn self-control, and get to know a variety of people.

In verse 4 of that chapter we read, "For it was so, when Solomon was old, that his wives turned his heart after other gods; and his heart was not loyal to the Lord his God . . . so Solomon did evil in the sight of the Lord" (verse 6). Solomon had been warned and he did not heed the warning. He let his emotions overcome what he knew to be right. He was judged for marrying women who turned him away from God.

There were women in the Old Testament, such as Ruth, who converted to Judaism and married men of a different race.

God created all of us, and that includes the color of our skin. He loves us all equally. It would be much more important to take into consideration the heart of a young man than the color of his skin. Does he love Jesus? Does he study the Bible? Is he a Christian?

And even after you have answered those questions you need to decide if it is expedient for you to date someone of another race. What do I mean by that? The word expedient means helpful, beneficial, or "something that is suitable for achieving a particular end in a given circumstance" (Mirriam-Webster, online).

Will dating someone of another race be helpful or beneficial? Understanding that you will eventually marry someone that you date, will you be just as happy for your children to grow up biracial? I have seen instances when a young lady started dating someone of another race, and there were those of her own race who were not interested in dating her after that. There will always be those who look at the race of the person a young lady dates rather then the character of the person. We understand that is a shallow attitude, but these are all things to consider.

The New Testament does not have any prohibition against dating someone of another race. God accepts all people no matter who they are. But every young lady will have to decide if interracial dating is wise, helpful or expedient for her.

When our boys were growing up, they completely understood that God loves all people, and Christians in particular, as His children. We lived in many places in the United States. Culturally speaking, interracial marriage was much more acceptable when we lived in Denver, Colorado, than it was when we moved to Blountville, Tennessee. We often told them that if they fell in love with a young lady of another race it would be a better life for them and their children if they lived in an area where it was more culturally acceptable. We have to live "in" this world, even if we are not "of" this world.

Any young lady who is considering interracial dating would be wise to talk with interracial Christian couples who are "living the life." What challenges do they face with their families, their communities and their daily lives?

One Person You Date Will be Your Mate

You will eventually marry someone you date. Dating provides an opportunity to build good character, strengthen your faith, learn self-control, and get to know a variety of people. The famous British leader of the 20th century, Sir Winston Churchill, said it this way: "Where does family start? It starts with a young man falling in love with a girl. No superior alternative has been found." And it never will be. Proverbs 30:18-19 tells us that one of the most wonderful things in this world is "the way of a man with a young woman." God made it that way.

Our oldest son Stan dated quite a bit in high school and was heading off to college. We discussed his plans and he made this comment, "Mom, I figure if I keep God first in my life and marry the right girl, it won't matter too much what else I do." He had the right idea!

Pray before you go on a date. Stay close to the Lord. One young lady told about a young man who picked her up for their first date. He opened the car door for her and then got behind the wheel. Before he started that car, he said, "Could we pray together before we leave?"

She was so impressed! She said her first thought was to say, "Yes, and I will marry you, too!"

Remember our definition of dating? It is the process of us becoming the right girl while we wait for the right guy. Wait for the guy who puts the Lord in the center of his life . . . just like you do, and choose wisely! Ask yourself about the person you are dating, "If my children grow up to be just like him, will they go to heaven?"

Questions
Chapter 9

1) What does it mean to glorify God in your spirit? How does this relate to dating?

2) What does it mean to purpose in your heart about the kinds of young men you will date and how you will act on a date?

3) Why do "hooking up" and "fwb" not mirror real life? Why can they not be defined as real relationships?

4) In his book Dateable, what comment does Justin make about "easy girls"?

5) What does this chapter say is the definition of dating? Do you think it is a good one? Would you change it in any way?

6) Why is it up to you to understand that you don't owe a guy anything just because you are dating?

7) What would be some "red flags" in your relationship with a guy?

8) How can you see the real person in someone you are dating by the way he treats waiters, waitresses and even his own family?

9) Why should a young man pay for your date with him?

10) Why is it important to listen to your friends some-times about a guy you are dating or that you think you might like to date?

11) What three choices does a pregnant teen have?

12) Why should you pray before going out on a date?

13) Why is it so important to date a young man with values very similar to yours and who cares about the Lord like you do?

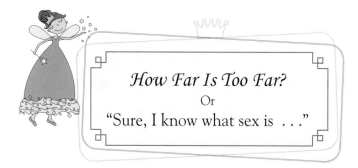

How Far Is Too Far?
Or
"Sure, I know what sex is . . ."

"For this is the will of God, your sanctification: that you should abstain from sexual immorality; that each of you should know how to possess his own vessel (body) in sanctification and honor, not in passion of lust, like the Gentiles who do not know God; that no one should take advantage of and defraud his brother in this matter, because the Lord is the avenger of all such, as we also forewarned you and testified. For God did not call us to uncleanness, but in holiness. Therefore he who rejects this does not reject man, but God, who has also given us His Holy Spirit."

I Thessalonians 4:3-8

I really couldn't believe this! Here I was, married for ten years with three children, and I was sitting in a required "sex education" class because I had decided to go back to college. The truth is, as they passed the banana and condom around, I couldn't help but think that this was nothing more than a "how to" class on sexual intercourse.

It felt like we were being programmed. For several days we studied every method of birth control. Of course we were never told that saying "no" was the best option. We were basically being taught to abstain from abstinence . . . the one thing that assured that we would avoid the dangers of premarital sex!

In our sex education class we never discussed relationships, commitment, setting boundaries or choosing to abstain. We never discussed how God made sex to be more than just a physical act. God designed sex to bring about an emotional closeness between two married people and because of that, a girl pays a high emotional price when the relationship is over.

This Dress is Pretty . . . but It's Used!

Sex is not the foundation for love but the expression of a love already respected, honored and cherished.

Imagine that I went into an exclusive dress shop to buy a dress because I was going to meet the President. I wanted just the right dress and I saw it hanging on a mannequin across the store. As I got closer, I noticed that a hem was coming loose on the sleeve. I also noticed a white spot on the skirt and it looked like someone had tried to wipe it off. It was smudged. The clerk said that the dress had been worn once or twice before but she thought it would still look beautiful on me. You know, I just didn't think so. I wanted the best dress I could find to meet the President. And guess what?

When a young man goes looking for a young lady to marry, he is not going to look for someone with lots of emotional damage. When a young man is looking for a young lady to share the rest of his life with, to be the mother of his children, the keeper of his home, and the love of his life, he is not going to shop in the bargain basement!

I have made that statement to thousands of young ladies and recently I decided to test it to see if it was old fashioned or if it was still true. I asked my son, who was the youth minister at a large congregation, to do me a favor. I asked him to go into his class of eighteen teenage boys that night and ask them how many of them wanted to marry a virgin. He was reluctant at first, but then he said he would. When he asked that question, how many of those eighteen young men do you think raised their hands? Every one of them! It made me realize that some of the girls they were dating at the moment were very likely not the girls they intended to marry.

What Does "Technical Virgin" Mean, Anyway?

Some young ladies use the term "technical virgin" when they talk about sexual status. Usually this means that a young lady has not been involved in a sexual act that involved penetration. Any other sexual contact is acceptable to them. A young lady who believes this does not understand that virginity is not a state of mind but it is a choice that you make to stay away from promiscuous sexual acts outside of marriage. Usually this is just an excuse to participate in sexual activity.

Studies have shown that people who are happiest about their sex lives are those who reserve sexual intimacy for marriage. If during the dating process you have become emotionally, spiritually and socially close, the sexual intimacy in marriage will be a very precious aspect of an already strong relationship.

"You May Kiss Your Bride"

Last summer a friend of mine who is a photographer was taking pictures at a wedding. The couple were Christians who had dated for two years. After the ceremony, the preacher said, "You may kiss your bride for the first time."

Now my friend did not think anything about this until the couple kissed. And kissed. And kissed. She was waiting to take a picture of the newlyweds as they walked off of the stage. Finally, she said, they turned and headed out of the building, holding hands and smiling. She said as soon as they got outside, they kissed again. She just had to ask them if this really was their first time to kiss.

The beautiful bride explained to her that she had decided that her limit for dating would be holding hands and a kiss on the cheek. For two years this couple had built a relationship on their love for the Lord and their love for one another. On a physical level, love included only holding hands and kisses on the cheek. When I mentioned this to one young lady she commented, "But what if she didn't like it?"

I can tell you this. After waiting two years to kiss a young man whom you respect and admire and one who loves the Lord and wants to take care of you . . . . you will like it! Guaranteed! God made us passionate people. He also expects us to control our physical passion outside of marriage. Inside of a committed marital relationship that passion can be unleashed and it adds to the foundation of the marriage. I often tell my husband that we were best friends before we got married, but we were not in lust until afterward. Passion for the man you are married to is a fantastic thing! And it works both ways!

I am reminded of a note that one little boy wrote:

"Dear God, I went to this wedding and they kissed right in church. Is that O.K.?" Neil

It is not just O.K. to kiss at your wedding. It was God's plan from the beginning. That is exactly where young couples should be kissing!

Marriage Is Highly Prized by God

God created sex to be a beautiful and enjoyable expression of love, but only between a man and his wife. The book of Hebrews tells us "Marriage is honorable (highly prized) by all, and the bed undefiled; but fornicators and adulterers God will judge"(Hebrews 13:4). Do you see the implication here? Sex outside of marriage is adultery and fornication.

With sex rampant in every form of our media including songs, television and on the Internet, most teens start to think that everyone is doing it. That is simply not true. Everyone is not having sex. There are many Christian teens (and non-Christians, too) waiting until marriage. It takes a strong, committed person not to give in to peer pressure. A young lady who loves the Lord has the strength of God to help her. When you stand up for your commitment to sexual purity you are keeping yourself from committing sin, and you may be giving others the example they need to do the same thing.

Not Much Hope for a "Practice Run"

Studies show that 60% of people who cohabitate (live together) before marriage get divorced, even though they used the argument that they want to "try it" first and see if it works. Many people in the world think that going into marriage you need experience. It's a lame argument. The Bible teaches that going into marriage you need commitment. Living together without commitment can never be as satisfying as two people living together who are committed to God and committed to one another "for better or for worse."

How much stronger will a marriage be when two people share the wonderful gift of virginity? When a young man can tell his wife, "I knew God was going to send you to me. I have prayed for you for many years. I loved you before I ever met you. I have waited for you and you alone." And then for you to be able to say the same thing back to him! Now there is a recipe for success! All of those times you thought you were passing up a "good time" could never compare to that kind of a relationship. Sex is not the foundation for love but the expression of a love already respected, honored and cherished.

Sex is a Big Deal!

Young people often say that sex is no big deal. Sex is a big deal. So many young ladies I have talked with would give anything in this world not to have given in to a momentary lapse of judgment. Sex outside of marriage carries a lot of spiritual and emotional baggage. You could ask any Christian young lady you know who has been sexually active and is struggling with the consequences. God made a big deal of sex in the marriage relationship because of the great spiritual and emotional consequences.

Within marriage, sex is a beautiful act that comes out of the marriage covenant, and it is more than just an action. Sex joins a man and a woman in one flesh and creates a physical, emotional and spiritual bond between them. God made us sexual beings so that we could enjoy the spiritual, emotional and physical unity of the marriage relationship. God wants us to delay our sexual gratification for marriage. He knows that will increase our joy in marriage and we won't have bad memories of other sexual experiences. Within marriage, sex is the consummation of "two becoming one." Outside of marriage it is "me" taking away a part of "you."

"You Can Never Be Like Me Again . . ."

Not long ago, there was a D.A.R.E. Officer in our county who told this story about his daughter at a PTO Meeting. He said that his daughter went to a state college and she was rooming with a girl she did not know before going there. The roommate was promiscuous and constantly nagged his daughter about still being a virgin. She teased his daughter by saying that she was surely the only virgin on their floor in that girls' dorm. After about three months, the officer's daughter had taken all she could stand. One night when her roommate was going on about how his daughter was not like everyone else, she decided she wasn't going to take anymore. She looked her roommate right in the eye and said, "I can go out and be like you any night that I want to, but you can never be like me again!" Her dad was so proud of her when he was telling this story. You could see him beaming. And you know what? Her roommate never teased her about her lack of experience again.

The officer's daughter was apparently a young lady who had set her limits. She was a young lady who knew her worth. She was a young lady that her roommate will never forget for all the right reasons!

Don't Fall for the Lie . . .Oral Sex is Sex . . .

I could give you statistics here that show that one out of four sexually active teenagers is now infected with an STD (sexually transmitted disease). I could tell you HPV is the most common STD in teenagers and condoms provide almost no protection against the infection. There will be fifteen million new cases of STD's this year. And yes. . . . oral sex is sex. Studies of sexually active teenagers have proven that sexually transmitted diseases are spread by oral sex.

I could give you many arguments from a health standpoint of why you should remain sexually pure. Remaining sexually pure absolutely protects you from the risk of pregnancy. It can protect you from emotional problems such as depression and low self-esteem. It will protect you from bad sexual experiences that can cause a young person to question why they would want to love a member of the opposite sex. Many practicing homosexuals relate a bad sexual experience with members of the opposite sex as the reason that they turned to members of their own sex. And playing around with sexual activity can make you really obsessed with it.

Look what the book of Romans tells us happened to people who were constantly thinking about sex:

"Therefore God also gave them up to uncleanness, in the lusts of their hearts, to dishonor their bodies among themselves, who exchanged the truth of God for a lie, and worshipped and served the creature rather than the Creator, who is blessed forever. Amen. For this reason God gave them up to vile passions. For even their women exchanged the natural use for what is against nature. Likewise, also the men, leaving the natural use of the women, burned in their lust for one another, men with men committing what is shameful, and receiving in themselves the penalty of their error which was due. And even as they did not like to retain God in their knowledge, God gave them over to a debased mind, to do those things which are not fitting: being filled with all unrighteousness, sexual immorality, wickedness, covetousness, maliciousness, full of envy, murder, strife, deceit, evil-mindedness; they are whisperers, backbiters, haters of God, violent, proud, boasters, inventors of evil things, disobedient to parents, undiscerning, untrustworthy, unloving, unforgiving, unmerciful; who, knowing the righteous judgment of God, that those who practice such things are deserving of death, not only do the same, but also approve of those who practice them" (Romans 1: 22-32).

These ten verses show the slippery slope of sexual immorality. Every young lady who loves the Lord and wants a happy marriage someday with the love of her life will do well to heed the physical health warnings of the world, as well as the biblical warnings against sexual immorality. However, now I want to share with you the most important reason why you should keep yourself sexually pure.

"How Can I Sin Against God?"

Remember the story of Joseph? I am sure you remember the coat of many colors. That coat is not really what the story of Joseph is about. Joseph's life was one of commitment to God even in the worst circumstances. He was sold by his brothers into slavery. It's a wonder he didn't turn from God then. I mean, how could a good God let that happen? Don't we wonder why God lets things happen a lot of times? I know many young people who would have lost their faith over that. But Joseph didn't.

The question really isn't "How far is too far?" The question really should be, "How can I be pleasing to God, respect myself and keep the trust of those who trust me?"

After Joseph was sold as a slave to Potiphar (Genesis 39), the Bible tells us that the Lord was with Joseph and made everything that Joseph did prosper. We are also told that Joseph was handsome in form and appearance (verse 6). Do you know what that means? Not only did he have a great face to look at, but his form (body) was great, too! No wonder the Bible tells us that Potiphar's wife cast "longing eyes" on him and asked him to sleep with her.

Now the important thing for us to understand is Joseph's answer to Potipher's wife. The Bible says that Joseph refused to lie with her. He said, "Look, my master does not know what is with me in the house, and he has committed all that he has to my hand" (verse 8).

Joseph is saying that Potipher trusts him. Joseph does not want to lose his trust and Joseph does not want to betray him. There are people who trust you in this life to do the right things. Don't betray them.

And then Joseph goes on to say, "There is no one greater in this house than I, nor has he kept back anything from me but you, because you are his wife. How can I do this great wickedness, and sin against God?"

Was Joseph Tempted?

Does it sound like Joseph was tempted here? I think so, because he asks how can he do this "great wickedness." It sounds like he is convincing himself, as much as anything else. But then he says . . . how can I sin against God? Knowing that he would be sinning against God is the final argument that keeps Joseph sexually pure. Even though the Bible says that Potipher's wife tempted him day after day, God gave Joseph the strength to resist. He will give you the strength, too. Remember Joseph when you are tempted, and ask yourself . . . "How can I sin against God?" Sexual immorality is sinning against God.

Are You Fleeing or Flirting?

Now let's consider this. If Joseph had stolen a few kisses while Potipher was away, if he had teased and played with Potipher's wife, if he had flirted with her often, if he had sat with her for hours and caressed her, do you think he would have been able to resist sleeping with her? You see the point I am making here. One thing leads to another. In order for Joseph to remain pure, he had to steer clear of Potipher's wife. There are people you need to steer clear of, too.

How Far is Too Far?

Girls are always asking me, "How far is too far?" Like there is one magic point where you cross the line and everything leading up to that is wholesome and pure. That is just not the case. You see, so many things leading up to sexual immorality arouse lust and desire and cause one to commit sin in their mind long before (or even without) the actual physical act of sexual intercourse.

The question really isn't "How far is too far?" The question really should be, "How can I be pleasing to God, respect myself and keep the trust of those who trust me?"

For me personally, when I was dating, holding hands and anything above the neck was my limit. Throughout the dating process, I stayed committed to that decision.

I vividly remember one day that tested that limit. It was the Saturday before Stan and I were married. We were moving some things into his apartment and ended up sitting and talking on his bed for some reason. He leaned over and kissed me and I momentarily caught myself lying on the bed. Was I enjoying it? Yes. Did I momentarily want to forget that limit? After all, we were getting married the next Saturday!

I realized that I was about to do something I had kept myself from doing for many years so that I could come to my husband as a virgin. So what if we were getting married the next Saturday. We were not married yet! I did not linger. I popped up and said, "I need to go home now." And I did. I hope you can understand how much more special that made my wedding day in every way! I want that for you, too. But you have to want it for yourself.

You have to make wise decisions for yourself about how far is too far. I know young ladies who have decided not to kiss anyone before their wedding night. That is a great choice! Then you never have to worry about going too far. God is present in your life. He will strengthen you in your choices to be pleasing to Him, just like he did Joseph. Be smart. Be true to yourself. And then one day you may give yourself completely, without spot or blemish to the one you love.

A Renewed Heart

What happens when a young lady sins sexually? She may feel that there is no hope for her to ever be pleasing to God again. It is true that she cannot become a virgin again, but she can receive God's forgiveness. Although she has made her future more difficult because of the choice she has made, God is ready to forgive her as long as she does not willfully continue in sexual promiscuity. God can renew her heart and help her with her commitment to refrain from being sexually active. No one wants young people to do that more than God does.

One of the young ladies I surveyed said this about her struggle with staying sexually pure: "Staying pure is my personal struggle. Many things are out there that seem like 'fun.' . . . Staying pure, both mentally and physically is hard, but with support from Christian people, it is possible."   Whitney

It is not only possible . . . but God expects you to stay sexually pure. Your future will be so greatly blessed because of it!

Questions
Chapter 10

1) Why do you think that saying "no" (abstinence) was never discussed in my sex education class?

2) Why is it so important for young people to know what the Bible teaches about premarital sex?

3) Why might a young man choose not to marry a young lady with lots of emotional and perhaps physical baggage from her sexually active past?

4) What does the term "technical virgin" mean? Is it an excuse to participate in premarital sex?

5) Studies have shown that the people who are most satisfied in their sex lives are those who reserve sexual intimacy for marriage. Why do you think that is? Do you think God knows that? Why?

6) What does Hebrews 13:4 tell us about sex? What does it tell us about sex outside of marriage?

7) Why do you think that people who live together before marriage are more likely to divorce than those who don't?

8) Why is sex a big deal? What are the possible physical, emotional and spiritual consequences of

premarital sex? How do these consequences compare to a young man and woman who come to their marriage in purity?

9) What are some reasons from a health standpoint for remaining sexually pure?

10) Why is it important not to betray the people who trust us?

11) Why is sexual immorality sinning against God?

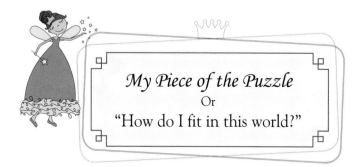

CHAPTER II

My Piece of the Puzzle
Or
"How do I fit in this world?"

"For we are His workmanship, created in Christ Jesus for good works, which God prepared beforehand that we should walk in them."

Ephesians 2: 10

Everything in this book up to this point has to do with who you are now, who you are becoming and what you want your life to be like. This chapter deals with the question: "Why?"

The first thing that you need to understand is that God created you. You did not come from "goo" as the theory of evolution suggests. I have heard the theory of evolution simply explained like this: "From GOO to YOU via the ZOO."

That is about the long and the short of it. There are plenty of books on Christian evidences available for you to study. These books will show you how much more believable it is that we were created by intelligent design than that we just evolved from some substance. (Scientists are not even sure what that substance might have been.) Let me recommend two books, *Out With Doubt* and *Matter of Fact*, published by Apologetics Press. They will present solid evidence to you that you are not descended from animals, that you have a soul that will exist for eternity and that you truly are made in the image of God.

"Get Your Own Dirt"

I like this story that I read recently. A scientist went to heaven and told God that He wasn't really needed anymore. Scientists were able to create life, reproduce stem cells, save lives and a host of other things that only God was supposed to be able to do. God looked at him and smiled. "Show me," He said. The scientist reached down and picked up a handful of dirt." God smiled, cleared His throat and said, "Get your own dirt!"

You see something really can't come from nothing. All of the machines, cars, computers, houses, buildings, cities, states and countries could not have come about by accident. All of them were created by architects, builders, craftsmen with intelligent design. Don't ever by blinded by the world's view of intellect. The Bible says that the beginning of wisdom is the knowledge of God and reverence for Him, but the fool says in his heart that there is no God (Proverbs 9:10; Psalm 14:1).

Why Am I Here?

I believe that every young person at some time or another asks, "Why am I here?" It is those young people who are never able to resolve that question who are a threat to society and to themselves. I have a pile of stories on my desk right now about young people who are shooting others at a local mall, at school, at church and anywhere else there is a crowd of people. I have read the stories of most of their personal lives. They have never come to grips with who they really are or what their purpose in life is.

> *God's hand is much bigger than yours or mine. He may have things planned for you that you cannot even dream of right now. Your responsibility is to obey Him, trust Him and look for opportunities to do His will.*

Most of them want to hurt someone (sometimes just any-one or as many as possible) because of the emotional pain in their lives. Some of them feel worthless. Some of them just want to go out in a blaze of glory mainly because they can't see themselves accomplishing anything else in life.

There are many adults who still question why they are here. Thousands of books are sold daily in bookstores around the world, because they claim to have the answer to this question.

It Really Is All About You!

Let me share some awesome news with you. The whole world is here because of YOU! God always knew that He would create man. Jesus says that God loved Him before the foundation of the world (John 17:24). God knew that we would not be able to live sinless lives and that He would have to send His Son to this earth. We are told that God chose us to be adopted as His children before the foundation of the world (Ephesians 1: 3-6).

177

The Bible tells us that before the foundation of the world God planned to send His Son. So God created the world so that we would have the opportunity to know and love His Son and be baptized into Him so that we could spend eternity in heaven. Isn't that awesome stuff? So you see, it really is about YOU, after all!

When you begin to wonder what your purpose in life is, remember that this whole world was created for you, and Jesus died for you. If you had been the only person in the world, God would have done that for you!

Your purpose in this life, the reason that God put you here, was for you to do God's will. We are told in Philippians, "For it is God who works in you both to will and to do for His good pleasure" (2:13).

You Were Created To Do Good Things!

Let me tell you this: big girls don't whine! As you mature physically, emotionally and spiritually, decide right now that you are going to accept responsibility for the choices you make.

You are God's workmanship. You were created to do good works. What are those good works? You don't have to go far to find out. The Word of God tells us about many opportunities to serve Him and our fellow men. We are told to live like Christ so that others can see Christ living in us. We are told to teach. Are you helping teach a children's class in your congregation? Why not? Have you been on a mission trip? Why not? We are told to visit widows and take care of orphans. Are you doing that? Sometimes women in the church focus on the things that we are not called to do, rather than being busy doing the hundreds of things God has called us to do! God may use you to be a leader of other women when you learn to do that.

After I was baptized, I began to focus on God's purpose in my life as a Christian wife and mother. Since then, God has used me to share that life and His Word with others. Every time I am in another country or in some other beautiful state sharing the truth of God's Word, I am amazed at the life God has blessed me with.

I realize that it all happened by the providence of God. The Bible teaches that when you become a Christian, your Christianity is everything about your life or it is nothing. God does not respect the lukewarm Christian life (Revelation 3: 15-16).

Your Handful or His?

I have seen the lives of strong Christian women that remind me of the story about a little boy who went into the general store with his father many years ago. It was a time when the candy was sitting around the cash register in barrels. When the father and son got ready to leave, the store owner told the little boy to put his hand in the barrel and take out a handful of candy. The little boy looked at his father and smiled but he did not put his hand in the barrel.

The store keeper said "Go ahead. It's all right." The young boy just looked at his father again and finally his dad scooped up a handful of candy and they walked out of the store. When they had walked a little way, the father asked, "Son, why didn't you put your hand in and take the candy?"

The little boy smiled. "I knew your hand was much bigger than mine!"

God's hand is much bigger than yours or mine. He may have things planned for you that you cannot even dream of right now. Your responsibility is to obey Him, trust Him and look for opportunities to do His will.

In case you doubt that God has big plans for you, let's read about how He created you and has laid out the plans for the days of your life.

"For you formed my inward parts;

You covered me in my mother's womb.

I will praise you, for I am fearfully and wonderfully made.

Marvelous are your works,

And that my soul knows very well.

My frame was not hidden from You,

When I was made in secret,

And skillfully wrought in the lowest parts of the earth.

Your eyes saw my substance, being yet unformed,

And in your book they all were written,

The days fashioned for me,

When there were as yet none of them.

How precious also are your thoughts to me, O God!

How great is the sum of them!

If I should count them, they would be more in number than the sand;

When I awake, I am still with you"

(Psalm 139:13-18).

Do you understand what these verses mean to you? God is thinking about you all of the time! He has plans for you just like He has always had plans for those who love Him. He tells His people, "For I know the thoughts that I think toward you, says the Lord, thoughts of peace and not of evil, to give you a future and a hope" (Jeremiah 29:11).

Your Decisions Determine Your Destiny

The problem comes when we let circumstances decide who we are going to become rather than becoming who we want to be because of our own choices. There are too many young ladies who want to whine and make excuses. Let me tell you this: big girls don't whine! As you mature physically, emotionally and spiritually, decide right now that you are going to accept responsibility for the choices you make. Decide right now that with God's help you are going to determine your own destiny. Decide that you are going to live your life with purpose and passion.

Our oldest son, Stan wrote this poem when he was a junior in high school. I think it reflects the attitude of every young person at some point in their lives:

THE PUZZLE

"Life is a puzzle,"
I pondered as I set to work,
Each moment like this crooked piece,
With all its little quirks,

Each piece may be a race I've run,
Or a sacrifice I have made,

Maybe it's a battle that I've won,
Or perhaps a prayer I've prayed.

When others look back on this picture
I've plaited,
I wonder what they will see.
Will it be an example of Jesus Christ?
Or a portrait of
A shallow
Selfish
Me?

By Stan Butt, Jr.

These thoughts bear some thinking about. Every day you are living your piece of the puzzle of life. Right now you only see the puzzle up to this time. It certainly isn't finished yet! Something very important for you to realize though, is that God sees the whole puzzle and knows how it is going to be completed. Your piece of the puzzle, as well as the puzzles of other people's lives, are going to be affected by the choices that you make.

Understand this. At different times in your life, you are going to wonder why certain things are happening. Why did your friend die? Why does your dad have cancer? Why are your best friend's parents getting a divorce? Why do your parents fight a lot? Why aren't you as smart or pretty as someone else? Why didn't you win the essay contest? (You thought your essay was good!) Why does the one boy you like never seem to notice you? Why do young people commit suicide? The puzzle of life sometimes looks pretty confusing.

The fact of the matter is that you are only responsible for one piece of the puzzle and its relationship to the other pieces touching it. You cannot control every piece of the puzzle. God is still in charge. Even Christ, when He died on the cross, said, "It is finished" (John 19:30). Had Jesus converted everyone? Had He healed everyone? Had He made everything in the world good? No. But He had done what He was sent here to do . . . His Father's will. And that is exactly what you were sent here to do!

Decide right now that with God's help you are going to determine your own destiny. Decide that you are going to live your life with purpose and passion.

Jesus was just one man. And yet for over two thousand years He has influenced the world more than any other person. Why? Because He did the will of His Father. That is your purpose, too. God is the only one who knows the influence you will have for eternity. How would it feel to be entering the gates of heaven and glance back and see someone you have influenced right behind you. What an awesome feeling it will be if that person looks at you and says, "Thanks," because you influenced them in some way to live for the Lord!

Becoming a Woman of God

You are on a journey now. On this journey your goal should be to complete your part of the puzzle by making your own piece of the puzzle the best it can be. You are growing from immaturity to maturity. You, young lady, are becoming a woman. The time will soon be past when others are making decisions for you. The time for self-absorption and fickle emotions will soon be gone. It is grow up time.

Mature young ladies begin making decisions based on what is best for everyone. A mature young lady is learning not to be selfish. She learns to care more about others than herself. She shows wisdom in making decisions and considers the consequences of her actions. She delights in being a good friend and takes responsibility for her own actions. A young woman who is maturing in Christ realizes that she is responsible for her own happiness and doesn't rely on what other people think to determine her value and worth. She studies the Bible. She prays. She controls her thoughts and does not let them control her.

The strong Christian young lady realizes that she is responsible for her piece of the puzzle of life. She understands that her relationships may enrich her life but they do not define her. She chooses to be defined by her relationship to God through Christ, and because of that relationship, she is free to be herself and live her piece of the puzzle with confidence!

Questions
Chapter 11

1) How does "Goo" to "You" via the "Zoo" explain the theory of evolution?

2) What does the Bible say is the beginning of knowledge?

3) Have you ever watched a building being built? How did it happen? What did this show you about intelligent design?

4) Why is it important for you to understand why you are here?

5) How can we know that God created the whole world just because of us? Is it really all about you?

6) Why were you put on this earth? (Philippians 2:13)

7) Talk about some of the many things God has called us to do according to His Word?

8) What does the Bible say about a lukewarm Christian?

9) How do we know that God knew us even before we were born? (Psalm 139)

10) Why do some people let circumstances determine who they become rather than making good choices for themselves?

11) What do you think the author means when she says, "Big girls don't whine?"

12) How is this life like a puzzle? How important is your piece of the puzzle to God?

13) When Jesus said "It is finished," in John 19:30, what did He mean?

14) Describe the characteristics of a mature young lady.

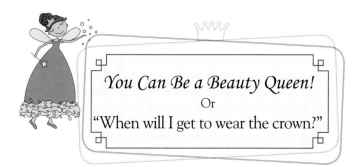

You Can Be a Beauty Queen!
Or
"When will I get to wear the crown?"

" . . . Be faithful until death, and I will give you the crown of life."
Revelation 2:10

Every now and then I turn on the television and see an advertisement for a bail bonds business in Nashville, Tennessee. It is called "Grumpy's Bail Bonds." The woman who advertises that she is the owner is Leah Hulen. She is a former Miss Tennessee. She has written a book entitled, "Pain Behind the Smile" in which she talks about her quest to be a beauty queen, and the way she abused her body and consequently her mind for many years. She talks about being in the depths of despair many times throughout her quest for different crowns. She thought each new crown would eventually satisfy her and make her believe in herself and her self worth.

Even after she finally won the title of Miss Tennessee and then Miss Tennessee USA she says, "My self doubt was incredible!"

"For me, the years of pressure to be 'pageant thin,' as well as some parasitic people who attached themselves to me just because of the Miss Tennessee titles, began to beat me down. I completely lost sight of real life goals, in exchange for the materialistic, short-term rewards."

She went on to say that "Leah, for all practical purposes, ceased to exist as an individual, or even as a person. I became poisoned by my unquenchable thirst for attention. And the more attention I received, the more I craved, until my body and mind responded to the constant pressure through intense and incessant bulimic bouts." When Leah did not win the Miss USA pageant she says her first thought was, "What was I going to do now to feel accepted by society and to prove that I was worthy as a person?" Leah did not understand that her true beauty and worth did not depend on winning a contest!

Being beautiful and smart in the eyes of God is the beginning of being a beauty queen forever.

The Battle of the Beauty Queens

In another instance, I was at the airport with a young lady whom I was taking to an eating disorder clinic. A beautiful young woman showed up as we were leaving with a dozen roses for the young lady I was taking to Arizona. When we got on the plane, I asked who the young woman was. The young lady told me that she was also a former Miss Tennessee who had battled and was still battling an eating disorder. She was married now and attended the same congregation as the young lady I was traveling with. Apparently, she and her husband were trying to have a child and her body was reacting to the many years of abuse. She miscarried each time she got pregnant. The young woman was trying to encourage this young lady not to let that happen to her!

Recently, Miss Illinois, 2005, was interviewed on Dr. Phil. She said, "Winning made me feel powerful, strong, invincible. After the Miss Illinois (American Queen) 2005 pageant I used speed to lose weight, because I struggle with my body image. There was so much competition, and I was scared, so I'd be taking these Adderral pills in heavy amounts, and then smoking weed on top of that to mellow me down. I started to realize that I needed all of the drugs at once: Vicodin, OxyContin, Xanax, Klonopin, Adderall, Ritalin, Valium, Lorazepam, crystal meth, crack cocaine, heroin – snorted and injected – deamphetamine salts, methamphetamine salts . . ."

This young lady started drinking at the age of 14. At age 16, she was drinking before school and at lunch breaks. At age 17 she was stealing Zoloft from her mother. At age 18, she started using speed to stay awake and lose weight and she tried crack cocaine for the first time. At 19, she started stealing to get money to buy her drugs. The department store where she worked had her arrested for stealing money and at that time she tried heroin for the first time. At 20, this young lady overdosed on Xanax and Adderall. Much of this was happening during her reign as Miss Ilinois.

At 21, she was addicted to heroin. At 22, this physically beautiful young lady almost died. Her father found her in the bathroom with a needle in her arm. She was an emotional wreck! Although she was now 22 years old, her emotional development and mentality was only that of a 14 year old because of alcohol and drugs. So much for the beautiful life of this beauty queen!

Do all beauty queens turn out having such a sad life? Maybe not all of them, but I can assure you that the ones I have known, who have put their faith and all of their efforts into worrying about how they look and whether or not they can win a beauty pageant, usually come to the end of the yellow brick road (just like Dorothy, in the Wizard of Oz). They find out that the thing they were searching for was a shallow, temporary fake that can never satisfy!

Beauty is Passing . . .

The Bible tells us the truth about beauty. Listen to the words of a wise man in Proverbs 31:30, "Charm is deceitful and beauty is passing, But a woman who fears the Lord, she shall be praised."

We are also told in the Bible that fear of the Lord is the beginning of wisdom. The word "fear" in this verse means respect for the awesomeness of God. What we learn from these verses is that respect for the Lord and His Word not only make you beautiful but also smart!

Being beautiful and smart in the eyes of God is the beginning of being a beauty queen forever. Colossians 3:2 reminds us to "Set your mind on things above, not on the things on the earth." When we do that, we will spend a lot less time worrying about how we look to the world and we will become much more beautiful in God's sight!

Lessons from A Real Beauty Queen . . .

A true beauty queen listens to others who know more than she does. As a matter of fact, she welcomes their advice, especially if she knows that the person genuinely cares about her.

Now let's see what we can learn from a real beauty! Her name is Esther and we have studied some things about her in an earlier chapter. Her story is told in nine chapters of the book of Esther. Please take time to read the entire book. Esther is a great example for us.

The Bible says that Esther was an orphan, stating that she had "neither father nor mother" (Esther 2:7). This verse also says the she was lovely (indicating her mannerisms) and beautiful. I seriously doubt if Esther was raised believing that she was a princess like so many of our young ladies are today!

Esther was raised by her cousin, Mordecai. When the king sent out a decree to find the most beautiful young maidens in the land, Esther was brought under the custody of Hegai, who was assigned to take care of the young ladies until the king would choose one of them to be his queen. Now here is an interesting part of the story. The Bible says that Esther pleased Hegai, and "obtained his favor; so he readily gave beauty preparations to her, besides her allowance. Then seven choice maidservants were provided for her from the king's palace, and he (Hegai) moved her and her maidservants to the best place in the house of women" (Esther 2:9).

I wonder why Esther became Hegai's favorite. Could it be because she was wise and not spoiled rotten? Certainly it was not because she flirted with him or granted him sexual favors. You see, Hegai was a eunuch (Esther 2:15). He could not have sexual relations with a woman.

We have also learned earlier that Esther was obedient to Mordecai. She trusted his judgment. Many beautiful young ladies today think that they know better than older, wiser people and it eventually causes them much heartache. That could have happened to Esther, but she chose to listen to and obey Mordecai.

Notice what happens when it is Esther's turn to go into the king. (Talk about competition!)

"Now when the turn came for Esther the daughter of Abihail the uncle of Mordecai, who had taken her as his daughter, to go into the king, she requested nothing but what Hegai the king's eunuch, the custodian of the women, advised."

If you are a faithful Christian young lady who is trying to live the Christian life, God's providence is working in your life, too. You are beautiful and worthwhile to Him.

Can you believe it? Here she is now getting ready to go before the king to see if she will be the next queen and she is listening to the advice of the king's eunuch! We wondered in an earlier chapter why she would do that? Could it be because he knew the king better than she did? Could it be because she was smart enough to trust Hegai's seasoned judgment better than her young inexperienced heart? A true beauty queen listens to others who know more than she does. As a matter of fact, she welcomes their advice, especially if she knows that the person genuinely cares about her.

As her story unfolds, we learn that Esther becomes queen and because of her position in the palace she eventually saves the Jewish nation from slaughter. When the time comes for her to act, she again listens to her uncle's advice. She prays to God and fasts for three days. She knows that she has a purpose. Her attitude is one of strength and courage. When faced with the possibility that she might die trying to save her people, she says without reservation, "If I perish, I perish!"

Esther Waits for God's Plan to Unfold...

The entire book of Esther and Esther's own life is a wonderful example of the providence of God. When Esther was an orphan with no father or mother, do you think she ever dreamed she would be a queen? When she was taken with many other young women to the citadel to prepare to go before the king, do you think she dared think she might be chosen? When she first went before the king by herself, do you think she might have been scared? When she went before the king without being summoned and was in danger of being put to death, do you think she was afraid? And during each one of these instances, do you think she saw the providence of God working in her life? The truth is, she could not have seen it until the end of the story, and most of the time, you won't either! Your life is like a video and God has already seen the end of it. All you can see right now is the snapshot you are living in—Trust Him. Wait for the end of the video!

But don't be afraid. If you are a faithful Christian young lady who is trying to live the Christian life, God's providence is working in your life, too. You are beautiful and worthwhile to Him. He gave His Son for you! Having three sons of my own, I can only imagine how hard that must have been. I have often wondered how our Father could have watched His Son die such a horrible death. He did it for you. Because you are beautiful.

Being Faithful is Believing that God Will Do What He Says He Will Do

God promises you a crown. It is a crown that will never fade. It is a crown that will not make you feel empty once you have attained it. It is a crown that will not leave you wanting more attention or looking for the next big competition. It is a crown that you will never have to give up!

And on your way to winning this crown, instead of drugs, alcohol and heartbreak, God will give you a life of purpose and direction. All He asks is for you to be faithful. That means you have to believe that God will do what He says He will do . . . and you have to live your life believing that!

Believe Him when He says, "Be faithful until death, and I will give you the crown of life."

Questions
Chapter 12

1) Why is the crown that a young lady receives in a beauty pageant just a materialistic, short term reward?

2) How can the craving for attention become habit forming? Why could this craving distort your life?

3) Why do drugs often become a part of the life of a young lady who is trying to be a worldly beauty queen?

4) What did Dorothy find out about the wizard when she got to the end of the yellow brick road? How can her discovery of the truth be related to young ladies who are striving for the crowns given for physical beauty?

5) What does Proverbs 31 tell us about beauty?

6) The Bible tells us in the book of Esther that Hegai was a eunuch. What does that mean?

7) Why would listening to Hegai be important to Esther? Do you think Esther was smart to realize this? Can the art of really listening to others help make us beautiful?

8) Why do you think that personal strength in a woman is beautiful? Do you think that guys are really attracted to a confident girl who can be herself and is comfortable in her skin?

9) Esther did not see the providence of God in her life until the end of her story. Sometimes we will not know at the time that God is working in our lives either. Why is this important for us to remember?

10) Describe the crown that God has waiting for us if we are faithful until death. How is it different from an earthly crown?

11) How are we to live our lives if we believe that God is going to do what He says He is going to do?

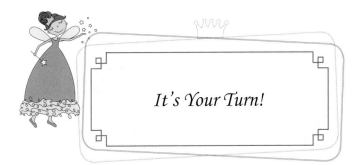

It's Your Turn!

"Let the words of my mouth and the meditation of my heart
Be acceptable in Your sight, O Lord, my strength and my Redeemer."
Psalm 19:14

Now it's your turn to reflect on what we have studied. There is room for you to write down something from each chapter that you want to remember or that can make a difference in your life.

Hopefully, many of you will have time to share these thoughts with the class. If you would like to share them with me, please make copies of these next pages and send them to:

Sheila Keckler Butt

P.O. Box 1283

Columbia, TN 38402-1283

I will use them to help other young ladies in the future. In the meantime . . . God is preparing your crown for you!

Chapter one

. . . Have you decided that Jesus is the first love in your life? Why or why not?

Chapter two

. . . I can glorify God as a daughter by . . . .

Chapter three

. . . I can glorify God in my body by . . .

Chapter four

. . . I can glorify God in my speech by . . .

Chapter five

. . . I can glorify God in my relationships by . . .

Chapter six

. . . I can glorify God in my recreation by . . .

Chapter seven

. . . What things can help me stay safe in the jungle out there?

Chapter eight

. . . I am deciding this about partying right now. . .

Chapter nine

. . . I will set my limits for dating as . . .

Chapter ten

. . . Is the question really "How far is too far?" . .
. . . What do you think?

Chapter eleven

. . . I am responsible for my piece of the puzzle of life. I want it to look like this:

Chapter twelve

. . . I want to be faithful until death because . . .